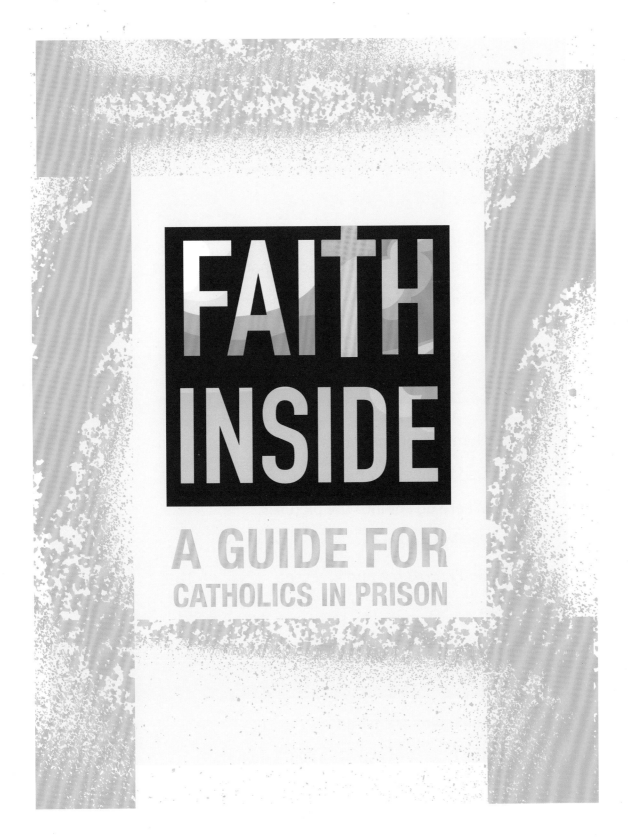

# FAITH INSIDE

## A GUIDE FOR
### CATHOLICS IN PRISON

FR EDDIE McGHEE PRISON CHAPLAIN

# FOREWORD

On my visits to prisons, I have been most aware of the important place that faith has in the lives of many prisoners, the time that prisoners have to reflect, and the vulnerability of those in prison.

All of you who read these words as prisoners will know how such matters affect you directly. This book has been written to help you: in your faith, in using the time you have to think about your situation and important questions in life, in allowing yourselves to be accompanied by Jesus Christ at times when you may well feel vulnerable.

I hope that you will find much in this book to assist you. It explains about the life of Christ, the Bible and the teachings of the Church. You will also learn of some of the great saints, about the Mass and how to answer some of the difficult questions people may put to you about the Catholic faith. All of these things can be of real, practical help to you as you lead your life, while in prison and beyond.

I am grateful to all those who have prepared this book, and I warmly commend it to you. I hope it will help you to turn to God with confidence at all times. And I assure you of my prayers for all those in prison, that they may experience the love and mercy of God.

*+Vincent Nichols*

**Cardinal Vincent Nichols**
President, Catholic Bishops' Conference of England and Wales

# WELCOME

A prison sentence can be a difficult time.
But it can also be a chance to make a new start
in life and move on.

## → Your journey

*Faith Inside* will take you on a journey. You will:

- Learn about how God works in your life.

- Understand who you are in a new way.

There are thirteen sessions which help you to explore your personal story and your faith. The starting point is where you are in your life right now – wherever that is.
Here are some questions to begin:

| | | | |
|---|---|---|---|
| ■ Was your family a church-going family? | ■ Did your family pray at home? | ■ Were there any obvious signs of being part of a faith community: a crucifix, a holy picture, or a crib at Christmas? | ■ If you have made your first confession, or have been confirmed, what do you remember about it? |

## → The story of Jesus

*Faith Inside* will also help you take a fresh look at the story of Jesus.

Sometimes when we hear about Jesus we become afraid that we can never meet his high standards.

But this should never leave us with a sense of failure. God loves you despite your failings and what you might have done in your life. We are all broken human beings.

We need to be honest with ourselves and recognise those times in our lives when our actions have been far from our best. We can't ignore our past. It is a part of who we are.

## → A faith journey

The journey of faith could be the most exciting journey that we will ever make. But it takes courage.

> We take the risk that we will discover things about ourselves and about our faith that will change us for ever.

We all find it difficult to change. We all have our struggles in life. This is part of being human. But the chaplaincy team is there to help and encourage you.

The writer G.K. Chesterton said:

**To love means loving the unlovable.**

**To forgive means pardoning the unpardonable.**

**Faith means believing the unbelievable.**

**Hope means hoping when everything seems hopeless.**

Doing time need not mean wasting time. It can mean discovering a new hope and sense of purpose. We can't change our past, but we can shape our future.

# What do we know about Jesus?

**All of us have heard *of* Jesus, but what do we know about him?**

**Perhaps we have heard or read many stories, but what was it like to *be* him while he lived on earth?**

## → Where did Jesus come from?

In Hebrew the word "Jesus" literally means "God saves". Jesus is the God who saves us. Jesus is God, but he became a human being in order to save all humanity from sin and death. Jesus became like us so that we might become like him.

Jesus is the Son of God, but he was born like any other human being. His mother was a young woman called Mary. Luke's Gospel tells us how the angel Gabriel was sent to Mary to tell her that she would have a child and that the child would be the Messiah, the one who would save Israel.

Matthew's Gospel tells us the same story with a slightly different slant. We are told how Mary was betrothed to a man called Joseph, but before they were married she was found to be pregnant. He was about to divorce her when an angel appeared to him and told him that Mary's child was conceived by the Holy Spirit.

Joseph agreed to become the foster father of Jesus and to bring him up as if Jesus were his own son. As a carpenter, he taught Jesus his own trade. This is why Jesus was known as a carpenter and as "the son of the carpenter".

When Jesus was around thirty he began preaching the Good News from God. However, his message did not go down well everywhere. The political and religious authorities saw him as a threat.

# → The trial and execution of Jesus

You might find echoes of your own life in the story of Jesus' arrest, trial and execution. We are asked to enter into a scene that looks more like courtyard than court. But it is a court, known as The Pavement, and it is the place of judgement.

- There is an accused – his name is Jesus of Nazareth.

- There is a judge – his name is Pontius Pilate. He is governor of this far-flung corner of the Roman Empire and has the power of life or death.

- There is a crowd – in the crowd are those who have accused Jesus. Jesus' friends are on the edge of it. They are interested but afraid. They are so afraid that many of them have run away.

- There are accusers – his accusers say he wants to be king. They remind the governor that there is no king but Caesar.

- There is a verdict – not wishing to appear disloyal to his master in Rome, Pontius Pilate, gives in to their demands. Jesus is condemned to death by crucifixion.

Once condemned, Jesus is paraded through the streets of the city of Jerusalem. Two other prisoners who will also be crucified are with him. Jesus struggles. Part of the indignity of crucifixion was that those condemned had to carry the cross on which they would die.

Jesus has been so badly beaten that he is already exhausted and near death. But the soldiers want to keep him alive so that they can carry out the death sentence. Someone from the watching crowd is forced to take part in this horrific ritual. He is told to carry the cross so that Jesus will survive until crucifixion. If he protested he might have been condemned too. The procession moves towards the gates at the edge of the city. The citizens of Jerusalem were used to processions like this. The Roman rulers often sentenced people to die. Jerusalem was busier than usual because it was near the feast of Passover. On the edge of the city, outside the walls, the three prisoners are crucified.

A notice with the reasons for executing each of the prisoners was pinned to each cross. On the cross of Jesus was written, "Jesus of Nazareth. King of the Jews." There was no doubt about the reason. Caesar was the only king. The message was written in Hebrew, Latin and Greek, so that visitors to Jerusalem for Passover could not doubt the power of Rome.

## → Deserted?

As he hung on the cross, Jesus cried out, **"My God, my God, why have you deserted me?"** This is not a cry of despair. The words are the first words of Psalm 22. Any Jewish person present would have understood that on the cross, in the impossible situation, Jesus was praying.

The prisoners were crucified and there was nothing more for the guards to do except wait for them to die. Usually this might have been a long wait. But the Romans were always careful about bad reactions from the people. The next day was Passover which was a sensitive time for the Jews. The Roman guards did not want the prisoners to die on the day of the Passover.

They broke the legs of two of the condemned men so that they would die more quickly. Jesus was already dead because he had been beaten so badly when he was arrested. They plunged a spear into his left side. There was no doubt that their work was done.

This looked like the end for those who had travelled with Jesus and for those who had hope he might be the Messiah. How could they know that they were moving towards the beginning?

## → My story

We have heard the story of Jesus and his encounter with the justice system of his day.

Behind each closed door in prison there is another story. My story. **Are there similarities in my story and in the story of Jesus?**

Before Jesus was arrested, tried and executed, he prayed.

**In my story what did I do?** There was a moment when I knew that I was going to court. I knew I might be going to prison. **On that very first occasion did I whisper a prayer, did I call on God?**

The journey to prison began for all of us in the same way. There was the moment that the court made its decision. No matter how we felt about that decision, no one was about to change it.

**Some of you may have been sent to prison many times, but how did it feel the very first time you were sent down?**

**As you waited in the cell at court after sentencing for the prison van, what thoughts went through your mind?**

**Did you pray then?**

**Was this prayer a regular thing or did you simply call on the God of emergencies for help?**

## Write a prayer

*Write a short prayer which asks God to help you in some area of need in your life. You don't need to use a lot of words.*

The poem below was written by a fellow prisoner. It may find echoes in your own very personal story. At the heart of the poem there is a moment when the writer turns to God in prayer.

## TRY

One step forward three steps back.

Inside out caught in a trap.

What goes up must come down.

Thoughts in my head going round and round.

Locked inside I can't be free

Yet trying to find my totality.

Is there light at the end of the tunnel

As I slip and slide inside this funnel?

Laugh or cry, scream or shout

Just don't know what life's all about.

Darkness seeps into the light.

Never seem to get it right.

On my knees I often pray

For something or someone to show me the way.

Work it out, that's oh so true

But it's easy to say when it's coming from you.

I hope one day it all becomes clear

And washes away my anguish and fear,

Cleans my spirit and soothes my soul.

I'll work it out, 'cos that's my goal.

➔ ## The sign of the cross
## – God is part of our lives

**When we make the sign of the cross we are acknowledging that God is a part of our lives.**

### In the name of the Father

We very simply acknowledge God as the Father of us all. We are God's children and loved equally. Your relationship with your human father may be good, bad at times, or non-existent, but God does not fail us as a human father can.

### And of the Son

Jesus is the Son. Jesus came on earth to point us in the direction of God as a loving father.

### And of the Holy Spirit

When the mission of Jesus on earth was over he returned to the Father. He sent the Holy Spirit into the world to strengthen and to encourage us on our own personal journey to the Father.

## → Talking to God

When Jesus prayed to God he spoke just like we speak to people we are close to. When his friends asked him if he would teach them to pray like this, Jesus gave them these words.

Our Father, who art in heaven,

hallowed be thy name;

thy kingdom come, thy will be done

on earth as it is in heaven.

Give us this day our daily bread,

and forgive us our trespasses,

as we forgive those who trespass against us;

and lead us not into temptation,

but deliver us from evil. Amen.

This prayer is called the Our Father. It shows us the important things that we should talk to God about. Jesus was telling his friends that anything and everything is OK to place before the loving Father. Nothing that we say or think or do is too small to be placed before God.

Hang up a copy of the Our Father in your cell where you can see it. We all have good intentions but sometimes a reminder is good.

There are other simple prayers that may help you. You can find them at the end of this book. We can always speak to God in our own words and in our own way. There are no rules or limits. God is always near to us. When we pray it brings us nearer to God.

➚ **The rosary**

**Using the rosary is another way to pray. We will cover it in detail later. Ask the chaplain to help you to learn how to pray the rosary.**

*Using a rosary, think of a special intention for each bead, such as for yourself, for a family member, or someone else.*

## To think about

*Where is God in your prison experience?*

*What keeps you going while you are in prison?*

**TALK TO GOD**

*Try praying the Our Father twice each day – once for yourself and once for someone you love.*

2

# I am called by name

### → Numbers or names?

**When you arrived in prison you were given a number. The prison number will stay with you for your whole sentence. In the prison system your number identifies you.**

During the twenty-seven years he spent in prison on Robben Island, Nelson Mandela was known as prisoner 46664. That number remains part of Mandela's history but it does not define who he was. Neither does your prison number define who you are.

When parents choose a child's name they are trying to say something important about this new child of theirs. And when we were formally given our name at our baptism this was a way of saying that we were unique in God's eyes.

How many member of the prison community have tattoos of their children's names? Or, if not their names, then their dates of birth.

### → God knows your name

God knows each of us by name. We are not just a mass of humanity. We are all God's children. As we saw in Chapter 1, God is our loving Father.

*What image of God do you have?*

*Do you see God as stern, or as loving?*

*How did you develop this image of God?*

*How did you imagine God when you were a child?*

In the Bible names are important. At the start of the Old Testament there is a story about creation. God names the man Adam and the woman Eve.

In another story, we find that when God invites a man called Abram to be a leader, he changes his name to Abraham.

King David is credited with writing the Psalms. There are 150 of them. Psalm 139 tells us something very important.

**O Lord, you search me and you know me,**

**You know my resting and my rising,**

**You discern my purpose from afar.**

**You mark when I walk or lie down,**

**All my ways lie open to you.**

It speaks to us about how God knows us.

## → Where do I fit into the picture?

We are not bad people. God does not create bad people. God creates people and then gives them the freedom to make choices. Sometimes we make the wrong choices. And others might be partly responsible for some of these bad choices we have made. For example, some of us might have been abused in our childhood, or not have been shown enough love by our parents. We might have experienced great emotional pain because of others.

Yet we need to remember that not all of the choices that we have made in life have been poor. We have also made good choices.

## → Feeling isolated

Even though God loves us and cares for us, sometimes we can feel isolated or cut off from other people. This poem, written by a prisoner, captures some of the feelings of isolation and frustration that can be so much a part of life in prison.

## WORKING IT OUT

I am trapped within
These four walls are my home now
Where I eat and sleep

Going to go mad
Need to calm down but can't
Going to freak out

I am never free inside
But my dreams are my freedom
Dreams will set me free

But I am never free
What can I do to help me
When there is nothing?

Feeling like nothing
Don't mean anything to anyone
Just got to move on

Need to find someone
Someone special to love me
To stand by me now

My life will change now
But I've got to learn the hard way
But I don't know how.

I will try my best
To change my life for the better.
I guess that will do.

# → God knows me and loves me

God loves us. The God of love calls each of us by our name.

When we are feeling low, this may be hard to realise.

We have to trust the message of Jesus. His whole life was designed to point us towards God our loving Father. He accepted crucifixion and death to show that even in situations that seem impossible, God is there.

There is a popular hymn which contains the line, "I have called you by your name; you are mine". There is a moment when your name is announced in court and suddenly you become the property of HMP. You are no longer a name but a number. It may have been a moment that brought you near to despair. It certainly would have touched your darkest fears. The hymn reassures us:

**Do not be afraid,**

**For I have redeemed you.**

**I have called you by your name;**

**You are mine.**

## God knows me and loves me

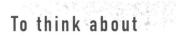

## To think about

*List five qualities that make you special.*

1

2

3

4

5

*What do you like most about being you?*

*What makes you feel free, even in prison?*

**TALK TO GOD**

*God, you know me
by my name. You
love me. Thank you
for believing in me.
Amen.*

# My invitation

## → The need for change

**Prison is a noisy place. Sometimes the noise can become almost intimidating. Sometimes the only opportunity for peace and quiet is to go behind your cell door. Even then, if you are sharing, it can be almost impossible to find peace.**

Time to reflect is always important. If we are to understand our faith, then we need time to stop and recognise the truth: God has a plan to change the world and has chosen me and invited me to be a part of it. God doesn't force us to change. Instead God provides opportunities to change.

*List five choices you have made during your life.*

*Were they good or bad?*

1

2

*What would you change and why?*

3

4

*What would you not change?*

5

# → The Bible – the story of God's invitation

The Bible is not a single book. It is a library of books, written by different people at different times over 1,500 years. It contains stories, poetry, songs, history and religious teachings.

We divide the Bible into two parts:

- The Old Testament, which tells the story of God's relationship with the Jewish people.

- The New Testament, which tells the story of Jesus and the birth of Christianity.

The stories in the Bible were written for different groups of people a long time ago. We need to think about who a story was written for to help us understand it. The Bible has been described as the story of how people did not grasp opportunities. The relationship between God and the Jewish nation is at the centre of the Bible. And often God's people, the Jews, like us, make the wrong choices. But God never abandons them.

Jesus constantly reminds the people that they have been chosen and that God will always welcome them back.

When you are released from prison you are beginning again. You cannot undo the past but you can move positively towards your future. We, like the people of God in the Bible, need to learn the lessons of our own history.

The message that Jesus gives is completely affirming. In God's eyes no one is unworthy. This is a very positive message for us. So often we find rejection and suspicion in society.

# ➜ Important Old Testament figures

## ↗ Abraham

Abraham began life as Abram. When God made a covenant with him – that he would become the father of the nation – his name was changed. He and Sara, his wife, were already old and childless. He was invited by God to leave everything and "go to a place that I will show you."

Because Abraham trusted God and went, he became a model of faithfulness to God's plan. This is one of the themes in the Old Testament.

Sara was childless and elderly, yet she gave birth to Isaac. It seemed impossible that this promise to Abraham could come true.

Here we see the God of the impossible situation. This theme will recur again and again in the Bible.

## ↗ Isaac

Isaac has two sons, Esau and Jacob. Esau is the elder of the two so he will inherit the birth right. However, Jacob deceives his father into giving it to him.

This story shows another key theme. God works even with those who are deeply flawed. This should be very encouraging to those of us in prison.

## ↗ Joseph

Joseph is the youngest son of Jacob. When his father makes him a special coat of many colours, his brothers are jealous and threaten to kill him.

Joseph's brothers sell him into slavery in Egypt, but he becomes an important figure there because he tells the pharaoh (the king) the meaning of the dreams he has. On Joseph's advice, the pharaoh stores up grain because there is going to be a famine.

When his brothers come to Egypt in search of food, they don't recognise Joseph at first. Eventually Joseph reveals his identity. He says:

> "Come closer to me." When they had come closer to him he said, "I am your brother Joseph whom you sold into Egypt. But now, do not grieve, do not reproach yourselves for having sold me here, since God sent me before you to preserve your lives."

## ⬈ Moses

Long after Joseph's time, his descendants are slaves in Egypt. A baby boy, the son of one of the slaves, is saved by the daughter of the pharaoh. His name is Moses and he is to become one of the key figures in the history of the Jewish nation. He was raised as an Egyptian in the house of the pharaoh, but he becomes the one chosen to lead his people from slavery to freedom.

This moment of liberation – what's called the Exodus – was just the beginning of their journey for the people of Israel. There wandered for forty years in the wilderness before they reached the Promised Land.

> Our own personal liberation from prison is our Exodus moment. We never emerge as the finished article. It is a new beginning. There is still much work to do. The realisation that we are valuable in God's eyes gives us endless incentive to continue with our own personal journey.

In the desert, God provided a leader – Moses. He was the lawgiver. He spoke with to God face to face on Mount Sinai when God gave him the Ten Commandments. They are to be the key for faithful living.

When Moses came down from Mount Sinai with the commandments, he found that the people had already turned away from their God and created an idol. They soon forgot about the God who freed them.

The people often forgot their God. Only a faithful few did not forget. The faithful few is another of the key themes in the Bible.

> At the heart of the Jewish tradition is the feast of Passover, which celebrates their Exodus from Egypt. The Jewish people see the Exodus as one of the key moments in the history of their relationship with God.
>
> Easter is our redemption and liberation celebration. We will understand it better if we understand the journey of the Jewish people.

### ↗ King David

Once settled in their new land, the people became comfortable. The people want to be like other nations. They asked for a king. David, a murderer and an adulterer, is their second king. Many of us will know the story of David killing Goliath with a sling and stone. In choosing David, God chooses the least likely.

### ↗ The prophets

As often as the people stray, God who has chosen them, calls them back. God calls them to return to faithfulness. He uses the voices of those that we now call prophets. Often the prophets did not want to do God's will. Three of the best known are Isaiah, Jeremiah and Amos.

The prophets didn't foretell the future. They invited the people to think about their actions in the here and now. If they did this honestly, they would understand that their actions now had a direct effect on their future.

They prophets also spoke of the day when the Messiah would come.

The prophets were maltreated and rejected. People did not want to hear the message. Their message was always to return to faithfulness. Only a faithful few would heed this call.

### ↗ Imperfect people

Moses and King David are two of the most important figures in the Bible. Yet they committed murder and adultery. Despite this, God chose them to carry his message to the people. God doesn't wait for someone to be perfect. He accepts us as we are now.

# → Redemption

Salvador Dali's *Christ of St John of the Cross*, which hangs in Kelvingrove Art Gallery and Museum in Glasgow, has become one of the most famous images in art.

*What does it say to you?*

*What does it say about God?*

The idea of redemption lies at the heart of the painting. Redemption means "buying back". To understand this, think of a pawnbroker. A pawnbroker gives a loan to someone in exchange for something of value. The person then buys the item back when they can afford to.

Jesus is the redeemer. He buys us back because we are valuable.

## Sean's story

Sean was speaking at an event in prison about his work placement. He was working for an organisation that refurbished old furniture to give to the most needy people in the community. He spoke of this work as "buying back a bit of his soul".

Sean's job was sanding the furniture. He didn't deny it could be boring at times, but he chose to see the end result of his work. He felt that what he did helped people. His work was valuable and so was he.

## ↗ I am valuable

How often have we been told that we are worthless? So often that many of us will believe it. In God's eyes it can never be true.

But God is not an indulgent father. He creates us, chooses us, and then invites us to achieve our potential. God does not condemn or reject us because we fail from time to time. Instead he invites us to recognise the times that we fail and to try and make a new start.

Are you familiar with kaleidoscopes? You look into a kaleidoscope and it produces all kinds of amazing patterns. It works by using mirrors and little pieces of coloured glass. Neither the mirrors nor the pieces of glass change, but the tiniest movement causes the pattern to change. Our lives are often made up of what can appear to be ordinary events. But it depends on how we view them. In the same way as a kaleidoscope, even the slightest movement can change the pattern. Sometimes thinking about what needs to change in our lives can be frightening. All we need do is change one thing at a time and we are on the way.

## To think about

*"Two men looked out from prison bars. One saw mud; the other saw stars."*
*What keeps you going while you are in prison?*

*What does this mean in your life?*

*Where do you find hope?*

*What is your hope for the future?*

## Why not try...

*Could you make a prayer space in your cell, even if you share with someone else?*

**TALK
TO GOD**

*Lord, be with me.*
*Love me.*
*Let me love you.*
*Amen.*

# Called to belong

## → The Church

**The *Catechism of the Catholic Church* speaks of the origin of the Church: "The Church is born primarily of Christ's total self-giving... by the blood and water which flowed from the open side of the crucified Jesus. For it was from the side of Christ as he slept the sleep of death upon the cross that there came forth the wondrous sacrament of the whole Church." (765)**

The very first Christians were the followers of Jesus Christ – his friends the apostles. They followed him; they saw his mighty deeds and heard his powerful words; they met him again when he rose from the dead. Jesus, knowing that his community needed to continue after his mission was completed, appointed his friend Peter to be the leader of the apostles. Peter was by no means perfect; he let Jesus down, denying he ever knew him; but he loved Jesus and was sorry for the times he had failed him.

## ↗ From Peter – to you

Peter travelled to Rome where he led the new Church. He was martyred there for his faith around AD 64. We celebrate him as the first pope, and there have been over 260 popes since he died. They are called the Successors of St Peter, and each pope is the head of the Catholic Church on earth. He is often called the servant of the servants of God. The Pope is helped to look after the Church by cardinals and bishops, who are the successors of the apostles. Wherever you live, you will be part of the local church – it's called the diocese – which is cared for by a bishop who has been appointed by the Pope.

The local bishop is helped by priests to look after all the Catholics in his area. The priests usually work in parish churches, but some work in hospitals, in the army and, of course, in prisons. There are many other people who help the bishop in his work. There are Religious priests and sisters and brothers; there are deacons; there are lay people who are also committed to the outreach of the Church. The bishop has appointed the person who looks after the Catholics in your prison.

So, you can see that there is a real link between you and the bishop and through him to the pope. And the pope has a real link right back to Jesus Christ who put his friend Peter to oversee the Church. The opposite diagram explains the structure of the Church.

For all Catholics the Mass is very important, and the Church guides us in how to say Mass, what words we must use and what parts of the Bible we hear. If your family or friends are in a Catholic church on Sundays, whether it's just down the road or on the other side of the world, they are using the same words (but maybe in another language) and listening to the same prayers and readings as you are in prison. The Church is so much bigger than any prison walls.

## The Pope is

- the leader of the Catholic Church

- the successor of St Peter, the leader of the Apostles

- the highest teaching authority in the Catholic Church

- Pope Francis is the 266th pope since St Peter

## THE POPE AND YOU

*Can you think of three occasions when the Pope was a good leader*

- *In what he said?*

- *In what he did?*

- *In the way he met people?*

*Does the Pope have anything to say to you in prison?*

# → Where do I fit into the picture?

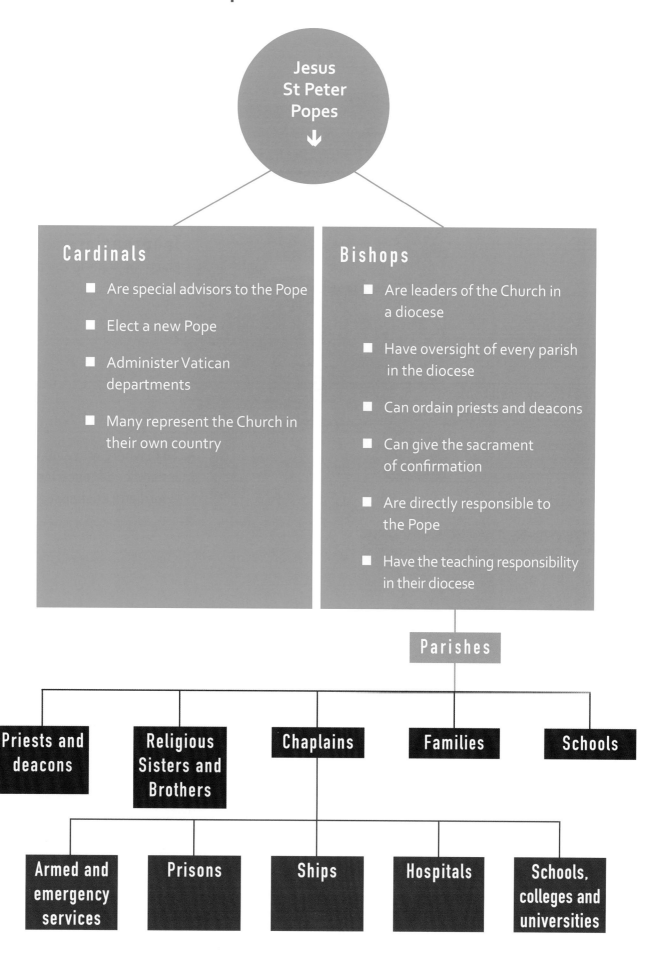

**Jesus
St Peter
Popes**
↓

**Cardinals**

- Are special advisors to the Pope
- Elect a new Pope
- Administer Vatican departments
- Many represent the Church in their own country

**Bishops**

- Are leaders of the Church in a diocese
- Have oversight of every parish in the diocese
- Can ordain priests and deacons
- Can give the sacrament of confirmation
- Are directly responsible to the Pope
- Have the teaching responsibility in their diocese

**Parishes**

**Priests and deacons**

**Religious Sisters and Brothers**

**Chaplains**

**Families**

**Schools**

**Armed and emergency services**

**Prisons**

**Ships**

**Hospitals**

**Schools, colleges and universities**

# → Inside a Catholic church or chapel...

**Crucifix:** Jesus' death conquered evil and gives us life

**Sanctuary lamp:** Jesus is present in the tabernacle

**Candle:** the light and life of Jesus and of our faith

**Tabernacle:** a resting place for Jesus in the Blessed Sacrament

**Missal:** book used by the priest when offering Mass

**Altar:** where we celebrate Mass and experience Jesus in his word and Eucharist

**Lectern (ambo):** where we proclaim the word of God at Mass

**Pictures and statues of Mary and of saints:** to remind us of their holy lives, to see them as our role models, friends and supporters in our daily life

**Lectionary:** the book which contains the scripture readings for each day's Mass

**Stations of the Cross:** to remind us of the suffering, death and resurrection of Jesus. There are usually fourteen stations but can be fifteen if they include the resurrection.

## Stations of the Cross

*Make a list of the stations of the cross in your chapel.*

*Put them somewhere in your cell: perhaps in your prayer corner.*

*Think about one station each day:*

- *What is happening to Jesus?*

- *Have you been in a similar situation?*

- *Who helped you?*

- *Pray: "I adore you, Lord Jesus Christ, and I praise you, because, by your holy cross, you have redeemed the world."*

- *On day fifteen, celebrate the resurrection. Make the day special in some way.*

- *Treat yourself and say thank you to Jesus.*

**Paten or Communion plate:** holds the bread (host) which will become the Eucharist, the Body of Christ

**Pyx:** used to carry Holy Communion to the sick

**Chalice:** holds the wine which the priest will consecrate during Mass

**Tabernacle:** (might or might not have a veil) – where the Blessed Sacrament is kept for prayer outside Mass and for taking Holy Communion to the sick

**Ciborium:** holds the Blessed Sacrament in the tabernacle and also for the distribution of Holy Communion

**Monstrance:** We can see and adore the Blessed Sacrament

# SEVEN SACRAMENTS: SEVEN OPENINGS TO LIFE

| Sacrament ⬇ | Signs and Symbols ⬇ | Meaning ⬇ | Important words and actions ⬇ | Effect ⬇ |
|---|---|---|---|---|
| **Baptism**<br><br>• Sacrament of Initiation<br><br>• Usual minister is a priest or deacon<br><br>• Is only received once<br><br>**1** | Sign of the Cross | Jesus' death on the cross conquered evil<br><br>We are "claimed for Christ" | • "I baptise you (name) in the name of the Father and of the Son and of the Holy Spirit. Amen."<br><br>• These words are spoken as water is poured over the candidate's head in the sign of the cross.<br><br>• In an emergency, ANYBODY can baptise someone provided they use these words and actions. | • We become members of God's family and Jesus is our brother.<br><br>• All sin is wiped away and we make a completely fresh start in life.<br><br>• We become members of the Church. |
| | Water | Cleansing from sin and impurity, new life | | |
| | Candle | Light of Christ, faith, life | | |
| | Anointing with chrism | The power of the Holy Spirit in our lives | | |
| | White garment | We become a new creation, our past sins are completely wiped out and we make a new start as a child of God. | | |
| **Confirmation**<br><br>• Sacrament of Initiation<br><br>• Minister is a bishop or a priest with the bishop's permission<br><br>• Is only received once<br><br>**2** | Renewal of baptismal promises and profession of faith | Declaration of intent to live as a Catholic for the rest of our life | "Be sealed with the Gift of the Holy Spirit." | • We are strengthened to continue the journey and mission we received at baptism.<br><br>• We become full members of the Church.<br><br>• We are empowered to be God's witnesses in our world. |
| | Prayer to the Holy Spirit | That the power of the Holy Spirit will fill the candidate | | |
| | Anointing with chrism | The Holy Spirit will inspire, lead and empower the candidate | | |
| | Laying on of hands | The Holy Spirit has set aside the candidate for a new mission | | |

| Sacrament ↓ | Signs and Symbols ↓ | Meaning ↓ | Important words and actions ↓ | Effect ↓ |
|---|---|---|---|---|
| **Eucharist**<br>• Sacrament of Initiation<br>• Only a priest has the power to consecrate the bread and wine, but a minister of the Eucharist does not need to be a priest or deacon.<br><br>**3** | Bread<br><br>Wine | Jesus' Body<br><br>Jesus' Blood | "Take this, all of you, and eat of it: for this is my body which will be given up for you."<br><br>"Take this, all of you, and drink from it: for this is the chalice of my blood, the blood of the new and eternal covenant; which will be poured out for you and for many for the forgiveness of sins. Do this in memory of me." | • We receive Jesus, whole and entire into ourselves. At the same time, he enters into us and becomes part of our life.<br>• We are united as Catholics in Jesus. (Many grains of wheat go to make bread, so we, although many, are one in Jesus.) |
| **Reconciliation**<br>• Minister is a priest<br><br>**4** | Sign of the cross<br><br>Sorrow for sin and intention to avoid sin in future<br><br>Extending hand over the head of the penitent | Jesus' death has conquered evil<br><br>Conversion<br><br>God's power and mercy have forgiven the penitent's sins | "I absolve you from your sins in the name of the Father and of the Son and of the Holy Spirit." | Sins are forgiven. |
| **Matrimony**<br>• The bride and groom are the ministers of matrimony. The priest is a witness on behalf of the Church.<br><br>**5** | Mutual consent of a man and woman to marry | Freedom to marry, to live together as husband and wife and to have children of their own should this be possible | The couple recites the vows: "I, (name) take you (name) to be my wedded wife/husband, to have and to hold from this day forward, for better, for worse, for richer, for poorer, in sickness and in health, to love and to cherish till death do us part. | "The two shall become one flesh." |

| Sacrament ↓ | Signs and Symbols ↓ | Meaning ↓ | Effect ↓ |
|---|---|---|---|
| **Holy Orders**<br><br>• Minister is a bishop<br><br>• A deacon can be in view of becoming a priest or can be as a permanent deacon who will not become a priest. St Francis of Assisi was a permanent deacon<br><br>**6** | Presentation and election of the ordinand | The community first says that the candidate has the right qualities before he can be accepted for ordination | The candidate becomes a deacon, a priest or a bishop and takes on a special role of leadership in the Church. |
| | Examination of the candidate | Public declaration that he shares the beliefs of the Church and understands the responsibilities he is taking on | |
| | Litany of the saints | Asking the saints for help | |
| | Laying on of hands | Empowerment by the Holy Spirit | |
| | **For bishop:**<br>• anointing with chrism<br>• presentation with the book of the Gospels, ring, mitre and crosier | Given a new mission and responsibility as leader and shepherd within the Church community in union with the Pope<br><br>Given the power to confirm and to ordain | |
| | **For priest:**<br>• anointing with chrism<br>• presentation with the book of the Gospels, paten, chalice and stole | Given a new mission and responsibility as leader and shepherd within the Church community<br><br>Can now offer Mass and administer the sacraments | |
| | **For deacon:**<br>• presentation with the book of the Gospels, stole | Given a new mission and responsibility to serve within the Church community<br><br>Given the authority to baptise, preach, and to administer Holy Communion | |

| Sacrament ⬇ | Signs and Symbols ⬇ | Meaning ⬇ | Important words and actions ⬇ | Effect ⬇ |
|---|---|---|---|---|
| **Sacrament of the sick**<br><br>• Any baptised Catholic who has reached the age of reason (usually around seven years old) can receive this sacrament if he or she is gravely ill and in danger of death; going for major surgery; elderly. It may be received more than once, even during the same illness if it progresses in seriousness.<br><br>**7** | Sign of the cross | Jesus has conquered all evil<br><br>Reminder to unite sickness and suffering with that of Jesus on the cross | "Through this holy anointing, may the Lord in his love and mercy help you with the grace of the Holy Spirit.<br>May the Lord who frees you from sin save you and raise you up." | • Forgiveness of sins even if the person is too sick to ask for forgiveness |
| | Laying of hands on the sick person's head | Calling down the power and strength of the Holy Spirit | | |
| | Anointing of the sick person on the forehead and palms of the hands with the oil of the sick | Comfort and strength, consolation and hope | | |

43

5

# Called to joy

**The characters in many soaps take on a surprising kind of reality in the consciousness of the public. When an actor dies, some people seem to feel a personal loss. Who is being mourned, the actor or the character he or she portrays?**

It is easy to confuse real life with what is happening in soaps. Characters in soaps can seem so real that we feel we know them personally and can identify with them. But we don't really know them.

The same is true of the characters from the Bible. We know their names and we even know some of the stories. But we don't know them.

Old Testament stories help us to understand the power of the relationship between God and his people. This relationship is deeply personal. We too, like Abram, are called to come and see for ourselves and enter into a personal relationship with God.

King David was a deeply flawed character who was able to turn his life around. David spent a large part of his life trying to atone for the wrong things that he had done. He has become a model for us all – another proof that God can and does use even the most flawed of characters.

This brings up some questions: What do we know about God? How do we get to know God personally, like a partner or a friend?

# → Our personal relationships

Let's look at our own lives. How do we create personal relationships?

We do it through talking to people and spending time with them. Relationships are about dialogue. And there are two parts to dialogue: there is talking and there is listening. Most of us are good at talking but not so good at listening.

Life is a series of complex relationships. Most of us have seen a spider's web. It is delicate and fragile and complex and beautiful. It is a mixture of space and of spun threads. The space is as important as the thread.

We are at the centre of our own web of relationships. We are joined in different ways to different people. We need to include God among these relationships.

If we call the Bible the word of God, then we need to listen to what it is saying to us. If we can do this we can start to make a relationship with God that is personal and unique.

At the beginning of a relationship we generally only let people know the things about us that we want them to know. We gradually reveal ourselves. We don't need to do this to God. God already knows us.

## → Getting to know God

But how do we know what God is saying to us?

We listen.

As with most things of value, we need to invest time. We call the time that we give to developing our relationship with God prayer. We all learned prayers when we were small but now as adults we are encouraged to use our own words.

We could think of the Bible as God's Facebook page. In the Bible there is lots of information and there are lots of "posts" and "comments" from other people that point us to a God who loves us. The more we look at the Facebook pages and post our own comments by praying, the more we get to know about God.

## Joy or happiness?

There is a difference between happiness and joy. What makes us laugh doesn't always make us happy. What makes us happy doesn't always bring us to joy. Laughter and happiness come and go. What brings joy is lasting.

Substance abuse is closely linked to this search for some kind of happiness. We confuse happiness and joy. We imagine that an ounce of this, a line of that, a bottle of the next is the key to unlocking life's secrets. It isn't, as we know to our cost.

## → Finding joy

All those who contributed to the Bible over the centuries are trying to tell us that lasting joy is only found in a relationship with God. It is only by developing this personal relationship with God that we become truly whole, and that we become fully ourselves. Wholeness and holiness are the same thing. If we don't have a spiritual dimension in our lives, then we simply cannot be whole.

When Moses encounters God at the burning bush he asks an important question, "What name will I tell the people? Who can I say sent me?" God gives his name, YHWH.
This revelation of the name of God is so special that it is never spoken by the Jewish people. We use the name "the Lord". God is saying to the people, "Here is my name: you can know me by this and we can develop a friendship."

When the Gospels begin to speak to us about Jesus, the announcement made by the messengers from God is, "I bring you tidings of great joy."

When we respond to the invitation to be on first-name terms with God we are on the way to lasting joy. It means that even in struggle and suffering there is meaning. We approach life differently if we know and are confident of God's love for us personally.

How do we develop prayer and conversation with God in our sometimes chaotic lives?

Jesus called God "Abba". This is a very familiar term. In our world it is the equivalent of Dad or Daddy. Some of us haven't had good relationships with our human father, but even so, we can have a very informal relationship with God.

We may feel insecure about this at first, so we may need some formal words. Praying the Our Father can help us.

# → The story of prisoner 16770

In 1939 at the beginning of the Second World War Maximilian Kolbe, a Catholic priest, decided to go back to his native Poland. He had been working abroad and Poland was under Nazi rule. He could have chosen his own personal safety by staying away from his homeland.

He ignored threats and intimidation, and tried to serve the needs of the local community, which included many Jews. Eventually he was arrested and sent to Auschwitz, the most notorious of the many concentration camps. He was given the prison number 16770.

Like many prisoners he was used as slave labour. When one of the camp inmates was found to be missing, the Nazis chose to execute ten men in revenge and to deter others. They did this by starving them to death. One of the men selected to die was Franciszek Gajowniczek, who had a wife and two children.

Maximilian Kolbe offered to take his place. He and the nine other prisoners were thrown into a punishment cell and left to die. After two weeks of starvation only four were left alive and only Maximilian Kolbe was conscious. The Nazis injected those surviving with carbolic acid to kill them. This was not because they pitied them, but because they needed the cell for further punishment. Maximilian Kolbe was executed on 14 August 1941. The man whose place he took survived the war and returned to his wife, but both children had died.

To those who were running Auschwitz, prisoner 16770 was just another con. Maximilian Kolbe had ceased to exist as soon as he was imprisoned in Auschwitz.

## → Faith can give us courage

Maximilian Kolbe's story shows all that we have been trying to say about God's love. It speaks about the presence of God in the impossible situation. It shows that very ordinary men and women are capable of the most extraordinary things if they have faith.

A strong relationship with God gives us courage to face the most difficult of challenges. Being a person of prayer does not mean that everything will suddenly be easy. That would be unrealistic. Being a person of prayer means that we can respond to each challenge with a confidence that it will not overwhelm us. We will emerge from our struggle strengthened and affirmed.

## To think about

*When was the last time you experienced joy?*

*Why was this?*

*Which people bring joy into your life?*

**TALK TO GOD**

*Lord, you know me better than I know myself. Be with me at every moment of every day. Amen.*

6

# Who am I to be chosen?

## → A deeper look at the sacraments

**Important moments in our journey of faith are marked by receiving one of the seven sacraments of the Church. The sacraments are the signs that God is involved with us at every stage in our lives in a very special way. Let's briefly look at them again.**

- Baptism – before we receive any of the other sacraments we must first be baptised. Our birthday is the day that we were born. Our baptism day is when we become members of the Church.

- Confirmation – in the sacrament of confirmation we are reminded that we are both chosen and strengthened by the Holy Spirit to meet all of the challenges that life presents us with and to use our gifts and talents for the building of God's kingdom.

- The Eucharist – in the sacrament of the Eucharist we are fed and nourished on the journey of faith.

- Reconciliation (confession) – the sacrament of reconciliation calls us to turn away from sinfulness and poor life choices. Each time we receive the sacrament provides an opportunity to make a new start.

- Marriage – the sacrament of marriage invites us to recognise and celebrate God's love for us in the love of husband and wife have for each other.

- Holy orders – the sacrament of holy orders calls men to the priesthood and to the service of the Church.

- The sacrament of the sick – the sacrament of the sick invites healing, both in body and spirit.

# → More about baptism

As baptism is the sacrament that makes us a member of the Church, let's look a little more closely at it.

You might remember watching a baby's baptism – perhaps that of your own child. An adult baptism is similar, making allowances for age. Parents and godparents make promises on behalf of the child, whereas an adult can speak on his or her own behalf.

*If you know you have been baptised but don't know the date, maybe it's time to find out.*

*If you know you have been baptised, do you know who your godparents are?*

## Symbols of baptism

A number of important symbols are used in baptism:

- Water – we need water just to be alive. It is the sign of life.

- Oil of baptism and chrism – we are anointed. We are chosen specially by God.

- The white garment – usually a white shawl or a specially-designed baptismal garment – is placed on the child as a sign that we have taken on new life in Christ.

- The baptismal candle – this candle is presented to the family with a reminder that they have to hand on the light of Christ to their child. We are the light of Christ in the world.

- The paschal candle – the paschal candle reminds us of the Easter event. New life and resurrection are key thoughts at this time. Jesus died but at Easter he was raised to new life.

## ↗ Baptism and responsibility

Baptism welcomes someone into the family of the Church, promising to offer the help and support needed to grow and develop an ever closer relationship with God. At the same time, the one who is baptised has a contribution to make to the spiritual health and wellbeing of the Church family.

There are key moments at the very beginning of this ceremony. Baptism is a request by the parents. It is a request made to the faith community on behalf of the child. With the request comes responsibility. "It will be your duty..." These are serious words. We have a duty towards our children. This is something we can't fob off.

Since baptism is routinely administered to children, it stands to reason that the thrust of the baptism ceremony is aimed not just at the person being baptised but at the family and at the faith community. Each one of us has a responsibility to the children that we welcome in baptism.

Baby X is blissfully unaware of what is happening. The family and the community need to accept their responsibility not just for the physical wellbeing of children but for their ongoing growth as people of faith who need to be nourished as they grow.

## ↗ What happens at baptism?

- The family want their child to be baptised,

- The child is welcomed into the family of the Church.

> "(name)... The Christian community welcomes you with great joy. In its name I claim you for Christ our Saviour by the sign of his cross. I now trace the cross on your forehead and invite your parents and godparents to do the same."

- We listen to God's word. This highlights the importance of the family and the faith community: children will never hear the word of God unless we expose them to it in both the family and the faith community.

- The minister speaks to those present about the importance of God's word and its significance for the person being baptised, for the family and for the faith community.

- The Prayer of the Faithful is for the person being baptised, for the family and for the community. Handing on the faith has three important components:
  - the individual and his or her choices
  - the family who help their child initially to grow in faith, and
  - the whole community

  These have two shared responsibilities:
  - to witness to the values of the faith
  - to support the individual in her/his growth in faith

- Litany of the saints: We ask the saints of the Church to pray for this child because they have already completed their journey of faith. Their example shows us that everybody has the possibility of growing in faith.

- Anointing with the oil of baptism (Oil of Catechumens) and a prayer for the strengthening of the child as she/he embarks on their journey of faith.

- The parents and godparents are invited to bring their child to the baptismal font holding the water in which the child is to be baptised.

- A prayer of blessing is said over the water.

- The parents and godparents renew their own baptismal promises and affirm the promises that they are making in the name of their child.

- The minister again ask the parents and godparents, "Is it your will that this child should be baptised in the faith of the Church you have all professed with us?"

- The child is baptised by pouring water on the child's head with the words, "I baptise you in the name of the Father and of the Son and of the Holy Spirit."

- We are again affirming our belief in the Trinity, that same Trinity which we acknowledge every time we make the sign of the cross.

- The baby is then anointed with chrism and clothed with a white garment. The baptismal candle, lit from the paschal candle, is handed to the family as the baby is usually too young to hold it.

- The rite of baptism ends with our family prayer, the Our Father, and the blessing of the parents in their new responsibilities towards their child.

## ↗ The Holy Spirit

After Jesus had been baptised, the authors of the Gospels tell us that the Holy Spirit came down on him. The presence of the Holy Spirit is closely connected with baptism. We also receive the Holy Spirit in the sacrament of confirmation and are sent out to use the gifts that the Holy Spirit gives for the building of God's kingdom.

> **Traditionally there are seven gifts of the Holy Spirit. They are: wisdom, understanding, courage, counsel, knowledge, piety and fear of the Lord. These may sound a bit abstract, but they show that the Holy Spirit works at every level in our lives and in the most unexpected places.**

## → Confirmation

The sacrament of confirmation focuses on the giftedness of those who have been baptised. In this sacrament, the candidates received the seven gifts of the Holy Spirit.

| Gift ↓ | Meaning ↓ |
|---|---|
| **Wisdom** | We see everything through God's eyes. So, for example, we love the world because God made it and not just because it exists. |
| **Understanding** | We make sense of the things we believe. |
| **Counsel** | We think before we act and learn how to stand up for what we believe. |
| **Courage** | We are able to stand up for our faith in God even if we have to suffer for doing so. |
| **Knowledge** | We look at our lives through God's eyes and try to see where God is leading us. |
| **Piety** | We want God to be first in our lives in everything that we say, think and do. |
| **Fear of the Lord** | We love God so much that we do our best not to commit sin. |

The sacrament of confirmation challenges us to discover our gifts and to use our gifts for the building of God's kingdom.

## ⬈ What happens?

The sacrament of *confirmation* usually takes place during Mass. The sacrament is a sign that each person, called by name, is specially and uniquely chosen by God.

- After the Gospel reading, the bishop addresses not just the candidates, but the whole faith community and speaks about the work of the Holy Spirit in our lives both as individuals and as members of the faith community.

- The candidates are then identified by name and called forward.

- The bishop leads a special prayer over those who are to receive the sacrament.

- Then the candidates are called forward individually.

- The bishop anoints each candidate by making the sign of the cross on his/her forehead with chrism. He speaks these words to the candidates using her/his given name in baptism "...Be sealed with the gift of the Holy Spirit."

- The bishop then exchanges a sign of peace with the candidate.

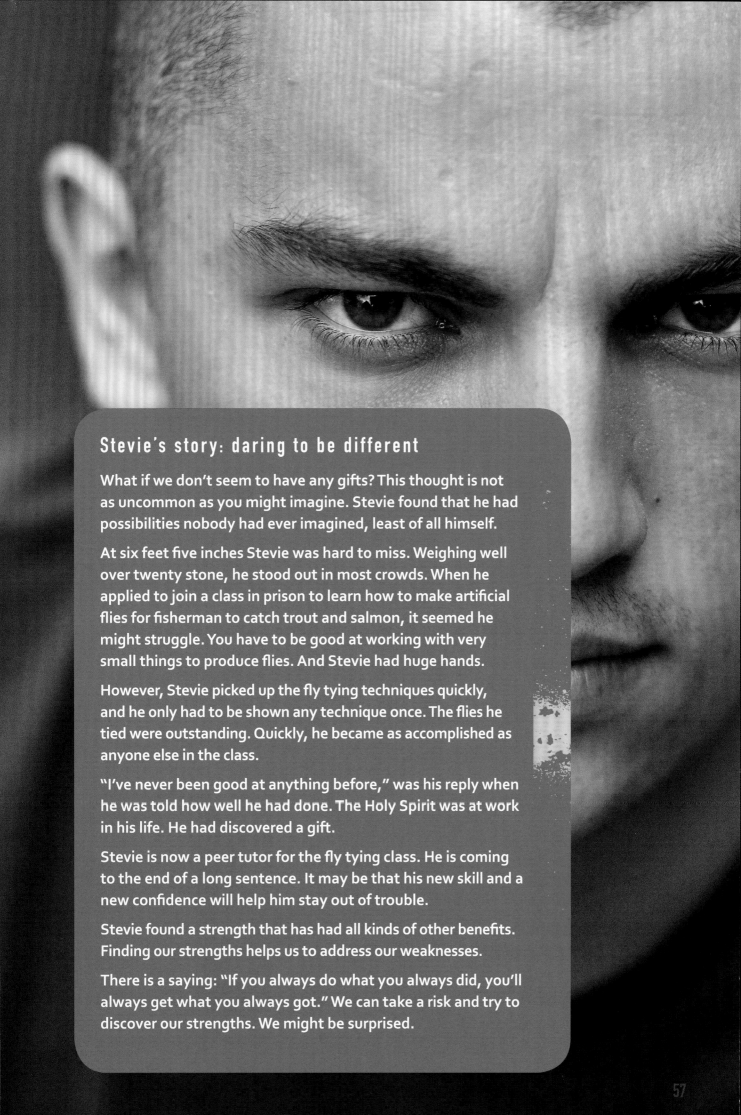

## Stevie's story: daring to be different

What if we don't seem to have any gifts? This thought is not as uncommon as you might imagine. Stevie found that he had possibilities nobody had ever imagined, least of all himself.

At six feet five inches Stevie was hard to miss. Weighing well over twenty stone, he stood out in most crowds. When he applied to join a class in prison to learn how to make artificial flies for fisherman to catch trout and salmon, it seemed he might struggle. You have to be good at working with very small things to produce flies. And Stevie had huge hands.

However, Stevie picked up the fly tying techniques quickly, and he only had to be shown any technique once. The flies he tied were outstanding. Quickly, he became as accomplished as anyone else in the class.

"I've never been good at anything before," was his reply when he was told how well he had done. The Holy Spirit was at work in his life. He had discovered a gift.

Stevie is now a peer tutor for the fly tying class. He is coming to the end of a long sentence. It may be that his new skill and a new confidence will help him stay out of trouble.

Stevie found a strength that has had all kinds of other benefits. Finding our strengths helps us to address our weaknesses.

There is a saying: "If you always do what you always did, you'll always get what you always got." We can take a risk and try to discover our strengths. We might be surprised.

## To think about

*What gifts do you have?*

*What gifts do members of your family have?*

*Who do you know in prison that has a special gift?*

*God called Jesus his "beloved Son".*
*How often do you think of yourself as God's child?*

**TALK TO GOD**

*Help me, Lord, to recognise my strengths and to thank you for your gifts.*
*Amen.*

# My journey of faith

### → Life's journey

Each of us is on a journey. There comes a moment in life when we are able to look back. There is also a moment when we can look forward.

Looking back means that we are aware of our own personal history. Looking forward means that wherever we have come from, there is somewhere we would like to be in the future.

### → At the crossroads

Wherever we started our journey from, somewhere along the way we have taken a turning that has brought us to prison. We probably look back with regret. Yet we can look forward with hope.

We can't change the past, but the future remains full of potential and is built on the choices we make today.

When God invited Abram to go on his journey, Abram had a choice. He could have said, "No thanks!" Instead he took the risk.

> The question that faces us on our journey is, "Am I prepared to take a risk, or will I opt to play safe?"

# → The journey of Jesus

The Gospels chart the journey of Jesus. His early ministry took place in Galilee, his home territory. He went from village to village bringing his new and dynamic message.

When he visited his home village of Nazareth, where he had been brought up, the locals were less than impressed.

> "Where did the man get this wisdom and these miraculous powers? This is the carpenter's son, surely? Is not his mother the woman called Mary...? So where did the man get it all?" And they would not accept him.

This response should have a very familiar ring. Some people like to judge us in a similar way.

That makes our journey difficult. It makes the potential for change even more difficult. But it's not impossible.

## ↗ Jesus' choices

Having journeyed locally, Jesus had a decision to make. He had to decide whether or not to head to Jerusalem. One of the key moments in the Gospels is when Jesus was faced with making this decision.

The story of this is generally given the name of the Transfiguration. It takes place on a mountain top, where Jesus is revealed as being in complete harmony with the Law and the Prophets. We see him talking with Moses, the lawgiver, and with Elijah, the prophet who is to return when everything is brought to fulfilment.

## ↗ Choices for Peter, James and John

The disciples, Peter, James, and John, are dazzled, blinded and confused. They know very well that if they embark on the next stage of the journey to Jerusalem there could be serious consequences.

Even in Galilee what Jesus had said and done had caused controversy.

Peter says to Jesus, "Lord, it is good for us to be here so let's make three places, one for you, one for Moses and one for Elijah."

But Jesus had made up his mind. He was going to Jerusalem. Now his friends had to decide whether or not they would go with him.

## ↗ What sort of friendship?

Peter, James, and John put their very real fear to one side and decided to take the risk and accompany Jesus.

Their worst fears were to be realised. Jesus did upset both the religious and the civil authorities in Jerusalem. Both groups needed him out of the way. They managed to bribe one of his friends, Judas Iscariot, to hand him over. They agreed on a price of thirty pieces of silver. The authorities arrested Jesus and his friends ran away.

Looking back, we might well ask, "What kind of friends were they?"

The quick answer is that they were the ones that Jesus hand-picked. Somewhere in the choices that he made there is a message for all of us.

# → The first followers of Jesus

So whom did Jesus choose?

A few fishermen initially. These were probably solid enough people, hard-working, devout in their Jewish faith, but ordinary men who did not stand out in any way.

## ↗ Levi (Matthew)

One choice was more dramatic. Jesus invited Levi to come and join the group. Levi was a tax collector. Tax collectors at the time of Jesus were among the most hated and despised people in the country. They were Jewish people exploiting their brothers and sisters. Yet Jesus chose Levi the tax collector to be one of his closest friends.

# → God rejects no one

There is a very simple message for all of us in the choice of Levi. No one, regardless of what he or she has done, is rejected in the eyes of God. This is one of the most powerful messages that you will ever hear. It is a hard message for those in prison who despise inmates who are on protection.

It is always easier to look at someone else and judge their offence than it is to look at ourselves and our own offending behaviour. We are asked to get honest with ourselves.

Some of us might struggle with some kind of an addiction. Breaking it is not easy, but it's not impossible. We should not despair. We can overcome our addictions, although it might take time. Addiction seldom comes alone. Addressing it means addressing our whole lifestyle.

The process of change may become scary. Anger may be your issue. Violent responses can be a way of avoidance. Whatever the reason for your present situation, an honest approach is a necessary beginning, because only then can you move forward with a sense of hope.

## Choice for change

*If we are honest with ourselves then it may mean that we need to make basic changes in our lives.*

*This is difficult.*

*What if you did decide to change?*

*What would you change?*

*Have you already changed the behaviour that led to you going to prison?*

*If not, do you believe you can?*

# → Role models on our journey

There are many examples of people who have turned their lives around after spending time in prison. Nelson Mandela is a role model, not because of the time he spent in prison, but because of the attitude that he brought to his freedom.

A generation earlier, Mahatma Gandhi led a protest against the British presence in India. He deliberately asked his followers to make their protests non-violent.

What Mandela and Gandhi had in common was a commitment to non-violence. Non-violence is often perceived as weakness, particularly in the world of prison.

We have many thousands of role models in our journey towards God. Here are some of our Catholic role models.

## ↗ Saints and martyrs

A saint is someone who tries to live a good and holy life. Some are officially recognised by the Church and are "canonised" (made a saint) by the pope at the end of a long and detailed investigation. Most saints are known only to God and the people whose lives they touch.

God calls each and every one of us to holiness so each and every one of us has a chance of becoming a saint and going to heaven.

In the canonisation ceremony, the pope says that so-and-so is "worthy of imitation": they are such good role models that, if we follow their example, we will also become holy.

A *martyr* is someone who is killed because of their religious beliefs.

Many saints and martyrs only became holy late in life after finding God and having a big change of heart. One definition of a saint is "the person who kept on trying when everybody else gave up" – and we can all try to do better, can't we?

## ↗ Some Catholic saints and martyrs

**St Peter:** He betrayed Jesus but was really sorry for his actions. Jesus forgave Peter, made him the first pope and the leader of the Church. Peter never again let Jesus down. The authorities caught up with him several times. He was repeatedly in prison but he refused to stop telling everybody about Jesus. Peter eventually annoyed the authorities so much that he was crucified upside down.

**St Mary Magdalene:** Tradition says that she was a prostitute but the Bible only says that Jesus cleansed her of "seven demons". She became a follower of Jesus, even to standing beside him at the foot of the cross. Mary was the first one to see Jesus after his resurrection and the one who took the good news to the Apostles. One tradition says that, after Jesus ascended into heaven, Mary Magdalene travelled to Ephesus with St John and Our Lady and lived with them until her death.

**St Francis of Assisi (1182-1226):** Francis was the son of a wealthy Italian merchant. He dreamed of becoming a famous knight, but instead was captured and imprisoned after a battle between Assisi and Perugia. He had a massive conversion and gave away all his (and his father's!) riches. He chose to live with nothing, or, as he put it, "in poverty, simplicity and joy". He tried so hard to imitate Jesus that he became "another Christ" and received the marks of Jesus' wounds in his hands, feet and side. His followers are called Franciscans.

**St Elizabeth of Hungary (1207-1231):** Elizabeth was a queen who had great love for people who were poor and marginalised.  She was only twenty-four when she died. One day, when her husband, Ludwig, was out hunting, he met Elizabeth carrying something. Thinking she might be stealing from the castle, he opened her cloak and instead of discovering the bread which she was taking to the poor, he found her arms full of roses. Elizabeth's husband died when she was only twenty. She used her inheritance to build a hospital, where she helped to nurse the patients.

**St Thérèse of Lisieux (1873-1897):** Thérèse's mother died of breast cancer when she was four-and-a-half years old. Thérèse became a Carmelite nun aged sixteen. She suffered greatly and died of TB, aged twenty-four. She had a great love for people in prison. She prayed so hard for a triple murderer that he had a big conversion and lived a very holy life until his execution in 1887. Countless prison inmates make St Thérèse their role model.

**St Nicholas Owen (1550-1606):** Nicholas was from Oxford and was so tall that he was nicknamed "Little John". He lived during the Reformation, when a practising Catholic faced possible arrest, torture and execution. A carpenter and builder, Nicholas made such good secret hiding places for priests that some are still being found today. He often used the aliases of Andrews and Draper. Nicholas was arrested twice, in 1594 and 1606. Although viciously tortured, he would not reveal the names of any of his Catholic colleagues. He died under torture in the Tower of London.

**St John Bosco (1815-1888):** John was an Italian priest who spent his life looking out for the no-hopers and refusing to give up on them even when everybody else did. Men and women who thought in the same way as he did followed John and became the Salesians. John's thinking was that, wherever young people were, that was where the Salesians should be. He had a special love for young offenders and came up with many ways of helping them to turn their lives around – including visiting a prison in Turin and talking the boys out for a walk one afternoon!

# ➜ Saintly prayers

Saints are simply people who have led good and holy lives and so are sure to be in heaven. Thinking about the life of a saint can inspire us to live in a different way. We can also ask them to pray for us. This does not mean that we are giving a human being the worship due only to God. Asking a saint for prayers is no different from asking a friend to pray for us.

A "patron saint" is one who, for some reason, has special importance. So, for instance, St Dismas, the Good Thief, who died alongside Jesus, is the patron saint of people in prison. We can ask him to help us to see Jesus even when life is at its hardest.

## ➚ The Prayer of St Richard of Chichester

*St Richard was a thirteenth-century Bishop of Chichester. He was hungry and homeless for two years because King Henry III, who wanted someone else to be made bishop, forbade people to give him food or shelter.*

Thanks be to you, our Lord Jesus Christ,
for all the benefits which you have given us,
for all the pains and insults which you have borne for us.
Most merciful Redeemer, Friend and Brother,
may we know you more clearly,
love you more dearly,
and follow you more nearly,
day by day.
Amen.

## ➚ Prayer of St Thomas More for good humour

*St Thomas More, a Londoner, resigned his position as Chancellor of England rather than go against his conscience. He was beheaded on Tower Hill on 6 July 1535 on the orders of Henry VIII. Thomas was a family man with four children.*

Grant me, O Lord, good digestion, and also something to digest.

Grant me a healthy body, and the necessary good humour to maintain it.

Grant me a simple soul that knows to treasure all that is good and that doesn't frighten easily at the sight of evil, but rather finds the means to put things back in their place.

Give me a soul that knows not boredom, grumblings, sighs and laments, nor excess of stress, because of that obstructing thing called "I".

Grant me, O Lord, a sense of good humour.

Allow me the grace to be able to take a joke, to discover in life a bit of joy and to be able to share it with others. Amen.

## ↗ From the prayer of St Padre Pio

*Padre Pio, an Italian Franciscan who died in 1968, became famous for helping people in trouble. In 1918 he received the "stigmata", the same wounds as the crucified Jesus.*

Stay with me, Lord, for it is necessary to have you present so that I do not forget you. You know how easily I abandon you.

Stay with me, Lord, because I am weak and I need your strength, so that I may not fall so often.

Stay with me, Lord, for you are my life, and without you, I am without fervour.

Stay with me, Lord, for you are my light, and without you, I am in darkness.

Stay with me, Lord, to show me your will.

Stay with me, Lord, so that I hear your voice and follow you.

Stay with me, Lord, for I desire to love you very much, and always be in your company.

Stay with me, Lord, if you wish me to be faithful to you.

## ↗ From a prayer of St Alphonsus Liguori

*St Alphonsus (1696-1787), the founder of the Redemptorists, spent his life helping the poor and marginalised. He had a special love for people in prison.*

My God, help me to remember that time is short, eternity is long...

Grant, O Lord, that I may love you always and never let me be separated from you.

O my God and my All, make me a saint! Amen.

## ↗ Prayer of St Ignatius Loyola

*St Ignatius Loyola (1491-1556) was a soldier who had a massive conversion and decided to fight for God rather than for earthly leaders. His followers today are called Jesuits.*

Dearest Lord,

teach me to be generous;

teach me to serve you as you deserve;

to give and not to count the cost,

to fight and not to heed the wounds,

to toil and not to seek for rest,

to labour and not to ask for reward

save that of knowing I am doing your will.

# True freedom

Freedom is not just freedom from prison. You probably think of that as the first freedom. We should be trying to establish freedom from whatever got us there in the first place.

## ↗ Fergal's poem

Fergal became part of a creative writing group in prison. It helped him rethink and express some very important thoughts. This poem of his may have familiar echoes.

When you become a prisoner of the State,
You learn how to survive; you learn how to hate.
It teaches you quick: you learn from it all.
You learn how to fight; you learn how to maul;
You learn how to stab; you learn how to slash.
You could take a man's life and not think it rash.

You start up innocent and end up a crook.
You don't even think about throwing a hook.
Violence is how you settle a feud.
It soon becomes a way to lighten your mood.
You start to enjoy the thrill of the fight.

You start to enjoy the kicks and the bites.
You start to enjoy the sight of the blood.
You soon let the anger wash over you in floods.

Before you know it, you've suddenly changed.
You start to do things way out of range.
You're full of anger and you don't know why.
You want to scream. You want to cry.

But you can't scream or cry because you're too full of hate.
That's my new life. That's what you learn
When you become a prisoner of the State.

You learn how to breathe; you learn how to talk.
You learn that when anger bubbles up, you go for a walk.
You learn that one punch will get you in the digger.
Down in the digger, you look at yourself,
The man you once were, a crumbling figure.
You've got a young son. You need self-restraint.
When that boy becomes a man, he'll know you're no saint.
Do you want him to grow and learn by example?
To teach his young mind that your violence is ample?
You want him to learn to punch and to stab?
For f*** sake man, you're meant to be a Dad.
I thought it was your job to teach him good from bad.
You need to buck up your ideas for the sake of the lad.

You'd better learn how to count up to ten.
Better to learn to channel your anger through the
medium of the pen.
You'd better learn to handle your anger and hate.
And you'd better do it now. Hey! Maybe it's fate
That you became a prisoner of the State.

On our journey through life, it is easy for us to get trapped in the blame game. The inadequacies and inequalities of life are always someone else's fault. The truth is that we live in a far from perfect world. We live in a world where there is much inequality and injustice.

Many of us in prison see "the system" as the problem. We see ourselves as victim. Others see those in prison as the problem. Fergal's poem paints a painful picture of a reality that we may need to face up to. It highlights that we have choices to make. It shows that it is possible to achieve great things.

## FOOTPRINTS IN THE SAND

One night a man had a dream. He dreamed he was walking along the beach with the Lord. Across the sky flashed scenes from his life. For each scene, he noticed two sets of footprints in the sand; one belonging to himself and the other to the Lord.

When the last scene of his life flashed before him, he looked back at the footprints in the sand. He noticed that many times along the path of his life there was only one set of footprints. He also noticed that it happened at the very lowest and saddest times of his life.

This really bothered him and he questioned the Lord about it. "Lord, you said that once I decided to follow you, you'd walk with me all the way. But I have noticed that during the most troublesome times in my life there is only one set of footprints. I don't understand why when I needed you most you would leave me."

The Lord replied, "My precious, precious child, I love you and I would never leave you! During your times of trial and suffering when you see only one set of footprints, it was then that I carried you.

Carolyn Carty

72

## To think about

*What one thing could you do today that is new and good and filled with hope?*

*Could it become a new habit for you?*

**TALK TO GOD**

*Loving Lord, help me to count to ten when I am angry. Teach me patience. Teach me love. Amen.*

# Turning life around

## → The Prodigal Son

**One of the best known stories of Jesus is called the Prodigal Son. A man had two sons. The younger son asks for his share of the inheritance he would receive. He gets the money and he heads out determined to enjoy life to the full.**

It is interesting to note that the father in the story does not sit the younger son down and give him a lecture before he gives him his inheritance. He allows the son the freedom to make the choices that he wants to make. He does not place any restrictions on the inheritance – he simply says, "It's yours, do what you want with it. "The son does what he wants. While he has money he has friends. We are told that while the money lasts he lives a life of debauchery. When he runs out of money he runs out of friends. There may be some familiar echoes in our lives as we hear this part of the story.

This young man who was once rich has lost everything. He is reduced to feeding pigs. He is starving and prepared to eat pig swill. No one is willing to give him anything.

He has reached rock bottom and begins to reflect on his life. He realises that he has made serious errors of judgement, so decides that he should return home and say sorry to his father.

When his father sees him in the distance coming towards the house, he runs towards him, clasps him in his arms and kisses him.

"Father, I have sinned against heaven and against you. I no longer deserve to be called your son," says the young man.

Instead of rebuking him, his father decides to put on a feast to celebrate his return. To the father it does not matter why his son has come back, only that he comes back. He has never stopped loving him.

As we think about our own situation, these words of Jesus should fill us with a sense of real hope. So often we will only have encountered rejection, anger, lack of understanding or compassion. When we put ourselves in the Father's hands we can expect forgiveness.

The elder brother, however, is angry. He has never put a foot wrong. He has always done what he should. He is resentful of the treatment the younger brother is getting.

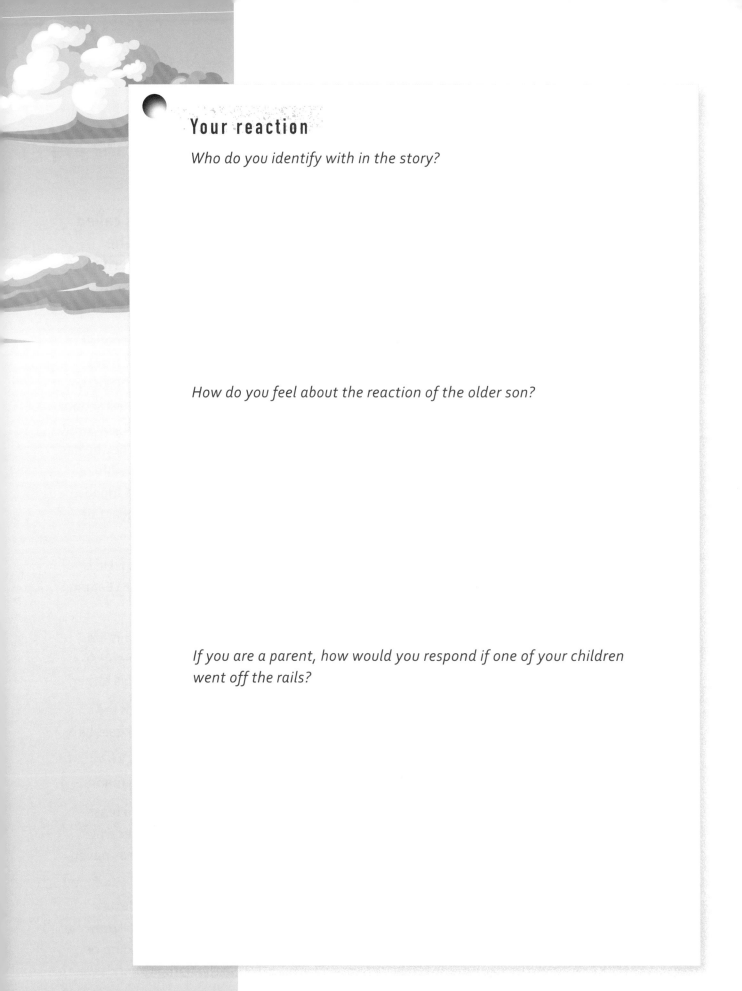

## Your reaction

*Who do you identify with in the story?*

*How do you feel about the reaction of the older son?*

*If you are a parent, how would you respond if one of your children went off the rails?*

## → Being forgiven by God

The father that Jesus tells about is a father who loves his children without any conditions. This is the image of God that Jesus wants us to understand. Just as we had a choice to make poor decisions, so we have the chance to turn our lives around.

God invites us to seek forgiveness and to begin again. The Church says that this moment is a special moment. It is called the sacrament of reconciliation, or confession.

Some of us will remember what we used to call first confession. We had to kneel in a confessional box and remember our sins.

Reconciliation means that I understand the consequences of my actions. I am actively prepared to do my best to change. I ask for forgiveness and I will try where possible to make amends for what I have done.

Our sins don't just damage us. They can also damage the people around us. The poet John Donne said, "No man is an island." He meant that our lives are closely linked to the lives of others. This can be either in a good way or a bad way.

An important part of the sacrament of reconciliation is that we must forgive ourselves. We are able to do this because we have been reassured of God's forgiveness. But it can be difficult.

Before we receive the sacrament we need to reflect honestly on our lives, just as the son did after he had wasted all the money his father gave him. The priest will be able to offer us encouragement to begin again.

## → Samereh Alinejad

In April 2014, Samereh Alinejad and her husband went to watch the execution of Balal, their son's murderer. "I stood very firm in my belief that I wanted him punished, so they didn't expect me to forgive," Samereh explained.

In accordance with Iranian law, Balal already had the noose around his neck so that she could kick the scaffold chair from under his feet. To everyone's surprise, instead of pushing away the support for her son's murderer, Samereh slapped him across the face and asked her husband to remove the noose. She then turned to Balal's mother, hugged her and wept with her.

One week after pardoning Balal, Samereh's life had changed. Through her act of mercy and forgiveness, she found peace. "Losing a child is like losing a part of your body. All these years, I felt like a moving dead body," she said. "But now, I feel very calm, I feel I'm at peace. I feel that vengeance has left my heart."

# → Eric Lomax

Eric Lomax had a fairly conventional and comfortable upbringing. He went to a good school and went to church regularly. As a young man he developed a passion for steam trains and for railways.

When it became obvious that Britain was heading towards war in 1939, he enlisted in the Army. He was sent to the Far East and became a prisoner of the Japanese after the fall of Singapore in 1942.

While a prisoner, he was a part of that group of soldiers who were to build the Thailand to Burma railway. When the Japanese discovered a radio and hand-drawn maps in the camp, he was identified as one of those responsible and beaten and tortured.

He was interrogated endlessly and beaten again and again when he failed to produce the answers they wanted. After one beating both of his arms were broken. He struggled simply to stay alive.

Only the care of his fellow prisoners, themselves in an equally desperate situation, helped him pull through.

Much later he wrote his story, called *The Railway Man*.

The story of Eric Lomax takes an unexpected twist. Years later, discovering that Takashi Nagase, one of his torturers, was still alive, he made the decision to go and meet him.

When they met, Eric, despite all he had suffered in the camp, found the inner strength to forgive him.

Takashi Nagase had to confront his own demons after the war as his actions began to haunt him. He came to realise that he should try to make amends for the awful things that he had done.

To atone for what he had done, he helped build a shrine near the notorious bridge on the River Kwai.

*Forgiveness is difficult. We talk about being able to "forgive and forget". The truth is that we might forgive but it is often hard to forget. It is a good idea to ask Jesus to heal our memories.*

*On the cross, Jesus prayed, "Father, forgive them for they know not what they do".*

*Do you think he found it easy to pray for his killers?*

- *Think of a time when you have found it difficult to forgive someone. Why was it difficult?*

- *Place yourself and that person in God's hands.*

- *Pray: "Loving Lord, forgiveness doesn't always come easy. You have shown me that I can learn to forgive even if it is only one step at a time. Forgive the people who have hurt me. Teach me to forgive them. Amen."*

- *Is there someone who finds it hard to forgive you for something you have said and done?*

- *Pray: "Loving Lord, you know that I am sorry that I have hurt other people. Watch over, protect and bless them. Stay with me and teach me to be kind. Amen."*

## → Pathfinding

You want to travel from London to Edinburgh and so you...

- might need a map and a compass or a satnav

- have a rough idea of the direction

- will avoid diversions

- make a choice to travel on foot, by bus, train, car or ship

## ↗ Pathfinding to God

If you want to travel towards God, you will discover that

- your map and compass or satnav might be
  - the Bible
  - the Church
  - role models

- you need to check your direction every day

- the road is not always easy

- shortcuts can take longer

- "scenic" routes might not be a good idea: you can get lost

- you first make a choice to travel towards God and then plan your best route – which might not be the shortest or the fastest road

The experts say that we make a "fundamental option" for God. In other words, we set our sights on God and start travelling the best possible way that we can.

## ↗ Diversions

Diversions are a hassle. They can be short so that you are quickly back on the right road, or they can get you completely and absolutely lost so that it is very hard to get back on track. Sometimes we land on the wrong road because we have been distracted or want to explore an unfamiliar town...

We can also find diversions on our journey to God. As someone once said, "It is hard to be good". Some of our sidetracks are minor: it is easy to return to the right path. Some are more difficult and we must try harder. We know that there is a right road: we just have to find it, however long it takes.

When our diversions on our route to God are deliberate, we call them sins. Some are serious and some are less so. There is ALWAYS a way back to God and ALWAYS the chance of forgiveness.

↗ **Five steps to finding the right road to God**

Recognise that you have taken the wrong turning.

Say "sorry" for the deliberate diversion.

Ask God for forgiveness in the sacrament of reconciliation.

Promise to try harder to avoid making the same mistakes.

Say "thank you" to God for forgiving you.

→ **Our Highway Code towards God**

Follow these and you can't go wrong.

■ The Ten Commandments, which God gave to Moses

■ The Beatitudes, which Jesus gave to us

# The Ten Commandments

**I am the Lord your God who brought you out of Egypt, where you lived as slaves.**

1. You shall have no other gods to rival me.

2. You shall not misuse the name of the Lord your God.

3. Remember the Sabbath day and keep it holy.

4. Honour your father and your mother.

5. You shall not kill.

6. You shall not commit adultery.

7. You shall not steal.

8. You shall not give false evidence against your neighbour.

9. You shall not set your heart on your neighbour's spouse.

10. You shall not set your heart on your neighbour's house or any of your neighbour's possessions.

# In other words...

1. Love God more than anything else and make God the most important person in your life.

2. Always say God's name with love and respect.

3. Honour the Lord by resting on Sunday and making it special.

4. Love and respect your parents.

5. Never hurt anyone or destroy their good name.

6. Always be faithful to your husband or wife.

7. Don't take anything that isn't yours.

8. Always tell the truth.

9. Respect someone else's marriage.

10. Be happy with what you have. Don't wish for other people's things and don't be greedy.

# The Beatitudes of Jesus

1. How happy are the poor in spirit: the kingdom of Heaven is theirs.

2. Happy the gentle: they shall have the earth for their inheritance.

3. Happy those who mourn: they shall be comforted.

4. Happy those who hunger and thirst for what is right: they shall be satisfied.

5. Happy the merciful: they shall have mercy shown them.

6. Happy the pure in heart: they shall see God.

7. Happy the peacemakers: they shall be called children of God.

8. Happy those who are persecuted in the cause of right: theirs is the kingdom of Heaven.

# Be – Attitudes

1. **Be respectful**: let God work through you.

2. **Be sorrowful**: grieving is OK. It shows your love.

3. **Be gentle**: it will get you further than you think.

4. **Be just**: the truth sets people free.

5. **Be merciful**: we all need forgiveness.

6. **Be pure:** open your heart and you will see God.

7. **Be peaceful**: everybody is a child of God.

8. **Be courageous**: dare to do good so God can work through you.

# Jesus summarised the Commandments and the Beatitudes

**He told us to love God and to love our neighbour in the same way that we love ourselves.**

## → Going to confession

There are many ways of doing this so you and the priest can be flexible according to the situation. There is a common basic structure but this can vary according to your needs. Don't forget: the only reason for the sacrament of reconciliation (confession) is so that you and God can, together, heal a damaged relationship. The priest is only the cable which connects you and God to each other.

We will now look at the stages of going to confession.

1.  On your road towards God, where did you:

    ■ start to doze and swerve onto the hard shoulder or into another lane?

    ■ speed up as the traffic lights changed to amber instead of slowing down and waiting until they changed to green?

    ■ drive through a puddle and deliberately splash a pedestrian?

    ■ roll down the car window and shout at someone who had annoyed you?

    ■ drive carelessly and puncture a tyre in a pothole?

    ■ run out of fuel because you hadn't bothered to check that you had petrol before you started your journey?

These are all examples taken from driving a car, but you can see where they might apply to your life journey towards God. Sometimes you might have been lazy and not tried hard enough. You might have lost your cool with someone – and so on. To give this thinking process its technical name, it is called the **examination of conscience**. You are looking at life to see where you might have done better.

2.  You go to the priest, face to face or in a confessional: the choice is yours. He greets you and prays for you to have the courage and strength you need to be open, honest and sorry.

3.  You might use your own words or you might say something like "Bless me, Father, for I have sinned. It is (say how long it is) since my last confession". If it is your first time, tell him. He will help you.

    Tell the priest how you have not been a champion driver on your road to God.

4. The priest will give you advice to help you to do better in future. He will also ask you to do something to show that you are sorry for your sins, such as saying a Hail Mary. He will then ask you to make an Act of Contrition (say sorry to God) as in the following example.

5. You might say sorry in your own words or you might say something like this. "O my God, I am very sorry that, through my own fault, I have offended you, who are so good. With your help, I promise to try not to sin again. Amen."

6. The priest will then raise his hand over your head as a sign of God's presence. He will pray for you, in God's name, forgiving your sins, in the words, "I absolve you from your sins in the name of the Father and of the Son and of the Holy Spirit. Amen. Go in peace." The priest might also ask you to pray for him.

And that's it! Going to confession in prison can be a liberating experience – and don't forget: the priest can NEVER repeat to ANYBODY the sins you have just confessed and he can NEVER take it out on you because he thinks you could have done better. If he does, then he has himself committed a big sin. This is called "the seal of the confessional". What is said there, stays there.

## To think about

*When was the last time you forgave someone?*

*What did it feel like?*

*When was the last time someone forgave you?*

*What does it feel like if you are unable to forgive someone?*

**TALK TO GOD**

*Loving Lord, teach me to forgive others as you have forgiven me. Amen.*

# Who do I want to be?

**"Food, glorious food! Hot sausage and mustard!"
The opening song from the musical _Oliver_
introduces us to Oliver Twist and to one of our
favourite topics, food.**

In _Oliver_, the song is, in fact, about the lack of food and the
terrible conditions in the workhouse.

Food is always a topic of conversation in prison. And there are
often complaints about its quality.

Even if we think the food is inadequate, we are unlikely to find
ourselves starving. In prisons in some countries it is up to the
families outside to provide food for inmates.

In prison the passing of our days is indicated more by the
rumble of the food trollies than by the hands of the clock.

## → Food for our journey

Our journey of faith requires spiritual food and drink. Just as
God provided food for the people in the desert in their journey
towards the Promised Land, so God now provides food for us in
our journey. This is the Body and Blood of Christ, which we call
the Eucharist and which we receive when we attend Mass.

The Mass recalls the Last Supper when Jesus shared a meal with
his disciples before he was arrested. When he shared bread
and wine with them he told them that they were his Body and
Blood. He also said, "Do this in memory of me." He invited
them to remember this moment every time they met together.

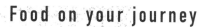

## Food on your journey

*What do you think the disciples must have thought when Jesus told them that they were to eat his Body and Blood?*

*What meals have been important in your life?*

*Why have they been important?*

# ➜ The feeding of the five thousand

The Last Supper wasn't the only time Jesus provided food. The story of Jesus feeding the five thousand is probably one of the more familiar stories from the Gospels.

When Jesus began his ministry in Galilee, moving from village to village, there were no televisions, newspapers or mobile phones.

The world that Jesus came into was predictable. Very little changed. Life had an even pace. People did not usually travel far from their own village. Someone local – Jesus was from Galilee – but with a new and different world view was a novelty.

He had established a reputation as a healer and as a preacher with something challenging to say. Jesus drew a crowd of five thousand, which shows what an impact his ministry was having in Galilee.

Even in the days when we have televisions, the internet and mobile phones, people are still prepared to gather in great numbers to see famous people.

A large number of people followed Jesus. They had heard the stories and they were eager to see what would happen. They wanted to discover for themselves if all that they had heard about this Jesus was true.

Once, as the day drew to a close, the disciples of Jesus were aware that the people must be hungry. They were hungry themselves.

They said to Jesus, "Send them away. This is a lonely place. There is nowhere to buy food and even if there were somewhere, we could not afford to buy it for them."

Jesus replied, "Feed them yourselves."

"Us?" They asked. "But... But... but..."

Andrew, one of the disciples, found a boy with five loaves and two fishes. Jesus blessed the food and to everyone's astonishment there was enough to feed all the people.

Just as God provided in the difficult situation in the desert, God is providing for his people in this difficult situation now. Jesus is not saying, "Look at me and see how wonderful I am." He is pointing the crowd in another direction altogether, the direction of the Father.

After the crowd had been fed there was still lots of food left over. The message is simple: God never provides just enough. When God provides, there is not only enough to go round – there is more than we could possibly need.

# → Passover

At the Last Supper, Jesus and his friends were doing what generations of Jewish people had done before and still do today. They were celebrating Passover, a very important event in the Jewish year. At Passover, Jewish people retell the story of their deliverance from Egypt and slavery with Moses as their leader. This is not just a statement about their past. It shows that God is in the midst of his people right now. A special meal was the centre of the Passover celebration. At the centre of the meal was the paschal lamb. The blood of the lamb, sprinkled on the doorpost, became the symbol of their liberation.

# → What is the Mass?

Much of the time we probably don't think much about it the structure of the Mass. It is worth looking at it.

- At the beginning of the Mass, we are reminded of God's goodness and generosity to each one of us. We then ask for God's forgiveness for those times when we have sinned.

- We listen to readings from the Bible, which is the word of God. The most important is the Gospel reading, when we hear about what Jesus did and said. In his homily, the priest tries to help us understand the readings and see how they relate to our lives.

- When we recite the Creed we state our belief in God and the teachings of the Church. This is followed by a few moments to pray for the needs of the local community and anyone special to us.

- In the second part of the Mass we prepare to receive the Body and Blood of Jesus. The bread and wine are brought forward by members of the congregation and the priest then consecrates them on the altar.

- Before we receive the Eucharist, we pray the Our Father and make the sign of peace with those around us. Shaking hands with someone reminds us that we are not alone in our journey; we are part of a community.

- At the end of Mass, we are blessed by the priest. Having been fed with the word of God and the Eucharist, we invited to share the Good News of Jesus with others.

## ↗ Not just a commemoration

At Mass, in a special way, we remember that Jesus gave us himself

- in his words
- by his actions
- at the Last Supper
- in his passion, death and resurrection

Before his arrest, Jesus told people "Unless you eat my body and drink my blood, you cannot have eternal life." People turned away because they thought he was telling them to become cannibals!

At the Last Supper, Jesus gave ordinary bread and wine to his disciples and said "This is my body... This is my blood... Do this in memory of me."

He gave them himself in the form of ordinary everyday food and drink to show that he is part of our ordinary everyday life.

Catholics believe that the Mass is not "just" a memorial meal. We do not say that the bread and wine represent Jesus in the same way as a photograph reminds us of someone we love. We say that they ARE Jesus.

When the priest says the words of consecration, the bread and wine become the Body and Blood of Jesus.

We cannot detect any change, but we believe that Jesus has transformed food and drink into himself so that, when we receive Communion, he comes into us and becomes part of us.

## ↗ The words of consecration

The words of consecration are the most important part of the Mass. Without them, there is no Mass.

"For on the night he was betrayed he himself took bread, and, giving you thanks, he said the blessing, broke the bread and gave it to his disciples, saying:

TAKE THIS, ALL OF YOU, AND EAT OF IT, FOR THIS IS MY BODY, WHICH WILL BE GIVEN UP FOR YOU.

In a similar way, when supper was ended, he took the chalice, and, giving you thanks, he said the blessing, and gave the chalice to his disciples, saying:

TAKE THIS, ALL OF YOU, AND DRINK FROM IT, FOR THIS IS THE CHALICE OF MY BLOOD, THE BLOOD OF THE NEW AND ETERNAL COVENANT; WHICH WILL BE POURED OUT FOR YOU AND FOR MANY FOR THE FORGIVENESS OF SINS. DO THIS IN MEMORY OF ME."

## To think about

*Today Jesus needs your hands, your feet, your eyes, your words to carry his love to the people around you.*

*Try:*

- Offering a word of encouragement or a smile to someone who looks unhappy.

- Giving a handshake to someone you haven't greeted for a while.

### TALK TO GOD

*Lord Jesus, I give you my hands to do your work.*

*I give you my feet to go your way.*

*I give you my tongue to speak your words.*

*I give you my mind that you may think in me.*

*I give you my spirit that you may pray in me.*

*Above all, I give you my heart that you may love, in me, your Father and all humanity.*

*I give you my whole self that you may grow in me, so that it is you, Lord Jesus, who live and work and pray in me.*

*Amen.*

# Health, sickness and dying

**The sixties were a time of great cultural change. It was the decade of the Beatles, the Stones and Bob Dylan; of flower power; of the Vietnam War; and of the assassination of John F. Kennedy.**

It was also the decade when drug-taking became fashionable.

Bert Jansch was an emerging talent on the folk scene in the 1960s. When the daughter of one of his friends died of an overdose of heroin, he wrote the song, "Needle of Death".

> When sadness fills your heart,
> Sorrow hides the longing to be free.
> When things go wrong each day,
> You fix your mind to escape your misery.
> Your troubled young life has made you turn
> To the needle of death…

The sixties saw the emergence of the drug culture that has since brought so much suffering to the lives of many people.

# → Addiction

Since the sixties many other substances have made their appearance, substances which have familiar names. We speak comfortably about them, but this is often a way of denying their addictive and destructive potential.

Substance abuse is part of the reality for many of us in prison. The challenge for us is find wholeness.

Here is a poem written in prison by Stuart.

I met her at a party. We loved it at the start,

Within three weeks of meeting her, she kind of won my heart.

I'd heard some things about her, some good things and some bad.

I was told not to trust her: she was cunning, sly and smart.

She made me feel so happy, so I pushed these things aside,

But soon things started changing, problems rushed in like high tide.

She made me borrow money, it didn't feel so nice,

But when I couldn't borrow she made me steal and beg.

And if I couldn't fund her she left me ill in bed.

See, what I didn't think of when I took her in my arms,

Was people tried to warn me that she would cause me harm.

So if you ever meet her, I'll tell you who she is.

Stay clear and do what I did and put her in the bin.

She's really very famous, stay clear of Heroin.

There are opportunities in prison to move towards being whole. The health team, the addictions team, and psychologists can all offer help. As well as this, the gym and the education facility can also help us change our lifestyles.

The Church also provides an opportunity to receive the sacrament of the sick. We shall look at this later in the chapter.

# → Parables

Jesus told a number of stories that we call parables. In them, he challenged his hearers to think differently about things. These parables contain important lessons about life and our relationship with God. We will look at two of them.

## ↗ The story of the Ten Lepers

In the time of Jesus, leprosy was a death sentence. There was no cure. People with leprosy were not allowed to live with the community. They were banished to live on the fringes of society and had to identify themselves as lepers if anyone came close. Lepers could only meet with other lepers. Being cut off from family, friends and the faith community led to them becoming isolated.

Jesus and his friends are travelling near the border of Samaria. Ten lepers stand some way off as Jesus and his friends approach. They call out, "Jesus Son of David! Have pity on us." Even in their enforced state of isolation they have heard of the stories of Jesus and the wonderful things that he was doing.

Jesus heals them but his response is significant. "Go and show yourselves to the priests." This was not strange. Jesus was obeying the Jewish law. Only the priests could give a clean bill of health to those who had been declared lepers. Jesus is telling the newly-healed men to do what the law required. As they headed towards the priests, they found that they were healed – but only one of the ten returns, praising God and throwing himself at Jesus' feet. He was a Samaritan.

Jesus asks, "Were not all ten healed? Where are the rest?"

The Samaritans were the near neighbours of the Jewish community. The Jews and the Samaritans loathed each other. For Jesus to identify a Samaritan as the one who returned praising God was to insult his own people. It challenged the way they saw their relationship, not just with God, but also with their neighbours.

"It is your faith that has saved you," Jesus tells the man. Jesus adds insult to injury. The Jewish people believed that they were the only people of faith. They thought their faith mattered more than any other. However, Jesus is stressing that personal faith, rather than an accident of birth, is what is important in our relationship with God.

Crucially in this story, the ten lepers themselves must start the healing process: they must recognise their need and ask for help. It is then that Jesus heals them.

# Healing

*What is most striking about this story?*

*In which area of your life do you need healing?*

*What prevents you from being healed?*

## ↗ The story of the Good Samaritan

Jesus' story of "The Good Samaritan" is so famous that the term, "a good samaritan" is used to describe someone who does an act of kindness.

A man is on his way from Jerusalem to Jericho when he is beaten up, robbed, and left by the roadside.

A travelling Levite and a priest see him lying there, but walk on by.

When a despised Samaritan sees the man, he offers first aid and brings him to the local inn, where he pays for his bed and board. He also asks the innkeeper to trust him that he will pay any outstanding additional cost on his return journey.

### ◌ Making sense of it

*What do you make of this story? Would you have passed by on the other side?*

*If you were a Levite or a priest, the chances are that you would have walked on. Why?*

As a Levite or a priest, you would have been on your way to help in the Temple in Jerusalem. To touch a bloodied and broken body would have made you ritually unclean and therefore unfit to meet your obligations in the Temple.

Jesus is telling his own people that even service in the Temple is no excuse for not helping your neighbour who is in distress.

The Samaritan understood this. The priest and the Levite did not.

There is a challenge for all of us in this story: to see a broader vision of God's interaction with all people. It also reminds us that we should never use God or our religious belief as an excuse for not helping a brother or sister in need.

## → Faith and healing

In the Gospel healing stories Jesus always highlights the faith of those who ask for healing. He points out that when we need help, especially when we are sick, we should turn to God.

Jesus is not saying there will be an end to sickness and death. Instead, he tells us that even in sickness and, ultimately, in our death, God is present, inviting us to new life.

In sickness, and as we move towards death, we can turn confidently to God our Father.

This does not mean that every time we pray when we are sick that we can expect a miracle cure, although it sometimes happens.

It means that we can ask the Father who loves us to heal us of our deep inner turmoil, of our anxiety and bring us towards a sense of peace.

We ask for reassurance so that we can understand and be comfortable with the truth that, even at the end of our lives, our journey continues into God's kingdom.

> **Do you know someone who is sick?**
> **Pray for them.**

## → The sacrament of the sick

In the sacrament of the sick, the Church invites us to recognise God's healing presence. It used to be called "the last rites". Some people still use that name.

The sacrament of the sick is not just for people who are dying. It is also given to people who are ill or anxious. Many elderly people receive the sacrament of the sick each year. If you are going into hospital for routine surgery, you can ask for the sacrament.

The Church wants to recognise our need to be very aware of God's presence whenever we are sick. It offers the sacrament to help us focus on God's presence in moments of crisis.

## ⌐ What happens?

The sacrament has some familiar characteristics.

We place ourselves in God's presence with the sign of the cross and with a prayer.

We listen to God's word from the Scriptures.

We are anointed with Oil of the Sick, firstly on the forehead and then on the palms of our hands, with the words, "Through this holy anointing may the Lord in his love and mercy help you with the grace of the Holy Spirit. May the Lord, who frees you from sin, save you and raise you up. Amen."

At the conclusion of the sacrament we are blessed.

The sacrament is usually given to people who are sick and are receiving care at home or in hospital. Typically, if the sick person is able to do so, they also receive Holy Communion.

## ⌐ In the parish

Nowadays, parish communities sometimes arrange special services that focus on their sick and housebound members. These services often include Mass and the sacrament of the sick. Parishioners often act as a volunteer taxi service to bring people who are sick and housebound to church.

There are several benefits to this:

- The parish community remembers that the people we pray for each week are real people and members of the faith community.

- Those who are sick or housebound are reminded that they still have a place and are a treasured part of the faith community.

- A little social event afterwards can help reinforce these ties.

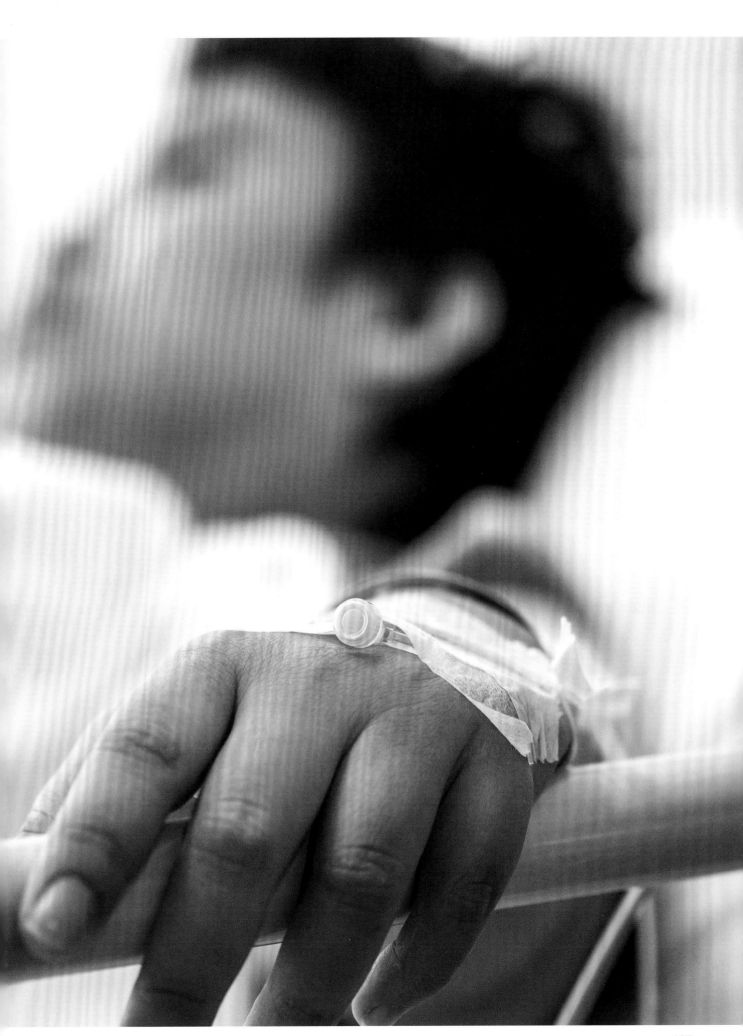

# ➔ Death in prison

Another aspect of prison life is the reality of death. When someone close to us dies while we are in prison this highlights our helplessness even more.

Our mortality is always something that we have to deal with. A death in prison or the death of someone close while we are in prison reminds us of this.

Sometimes the cause of death is suicide. Suicide is a source of trauma for everyone, both prisoners and staff.

## ↗ Lazarus

Death is the focus in the story Jesus told about Lazarus. When Jesus gets word that one of his closest friends is very near to death, he delays his visit.

When he arrives, Lazarus is dead and has already been buried for three days. Mary, the sister of Lazarus, is angry at Jesus. "If you had been here this would not have happened."

Jesus tells her gently that Lazarus' death will show the power of God. He raises Lazarus from the dead and calls him out of the tomb.

## ↗ God's power over death

When Jesus calls Lazarus from the tomb, he shows us that God our Father has power over life and death. God does not abandon even the dead, but instead calls us to new life. Jesus directs us beyond the obvious.

The story of Lazarus points us towards the death and resurrection of Jesus himself. It shows us God the Father's power.

## To think about

*Do you know someone who died in prison? How did you feel?*

*Pray for yourself and for the one who died, for the family and friends and for everyone in the prison who was affected by the death.*

## Why not try...

*Being extra kind to someone who has been bereaved and needs extra support just now.*

**TALK TO GOD**

*Lord of life, give eternal life and peace to everyone I know who has died. Comfort and strengthen the bereaved. Amen.*

# My family

**Who makes up your family? Do you have parents alive, brothers or sisters, a husband or wife, children? Perhaps you have aunts, uncles or cousins. Some of us might have a large family; some of us a small one. Some of us might have spent time in care. Whatever the case, we are all part of a family. And each one of us is created by God. God doesn't make mistakes.**

Some of us might come from a happy family. Some of us might come from a family which has experienced lots of problems and pain. No two families are the same. And no family is perfect.

## My family

*What does the word family mean to you?*

*Who are you closest to in your family?*

*How did your parents meet?*

*How important is family to you?*

# → The wedding at Cana

At the heart of every family is marriage. When two people marry they make a very public statement about human love. They are saying true love will last for ever. This is why Jesus chose to explain God's unconditional love for us at a wedding he attended.

Jesus, his mother Mary and his friends are invited to a wedding in a village called Cana. Although we are told nothing about the actual wedding ceremony, we know that there was a party afterwards. Weddings and celebration go together. Everyone hopes for a perfect day for the bride and groom. That means, however, that even a little glitch can seem enormous.

If this is true today, it was also true at the wedding that Jesus attended. When the wine ran out, this was a potential disaster and a source of complete embarrassment for the newly-weds.

Mary says to Jesus, "They have no wine." Jesus tells her that this is not their responsibility. He uses an unusual phrase: "My hour has not come yet." He has not yet officially begun his ministry.

Mary does not get into an argument. There is no hint of "I'm your mother and you will do what I ask you to do." Instead, without a sign of a fuss, she goes to the steward of the feast and tells him to do whatever Jesus might ask. She knows her son. He can't resist helping people in trouble, especially if the suggestion comes from his mother.

The focus of the story switches to the six stone jars. The jars are there meant for the washing that is part of Jewish ritual. Each could hold between twenty or thirty gallons of water. Jesus asks the servants to fill them to the brim and to take a sample to the steward of the feast.

When the steward tastes it, between 120 and 180 gallons of water has become not plonk but the best quality wine. He tells the newly-weds that they have broken with convention by serving the good wine at the end of the feast rather than at the beginning.

Jesus' friends saw this happen and recognised that he was more than just an interesting preacher who told good stories. Jesus was a question for which, as yet, they had no answer.

## ↗ God will provide

What are we to make of the story? Jesus did far more than save the young couple from the embarrassment of running out of wine. By providing more wine than the guests could possibly drink, he showed us that a loving and caring God never provides just enough. Instead we receive more than we could ever need.

## ↗ Together for ever

The marriage at Cana begins the public ministry of Jesus. He will later use the image of the vine and the branches when he speaks to his friends about loving relationships.

Jesus tells his friends, "I am the vine. You are the branches." They know what he means: they and their families probably grew and pruned their own vines and made their own wine.

Jesus leaves his listeners in no doubt of the very special relationship they have with him. He also tells them that, separated from him, the vine, they can do nothing: they are helpless and produce no fruit – and there can be no wine.

Our relationship with Jesus is the most important relationship of our lives. It is one which he expects to bear fruit. We might need pruning, but if we are good fruit, we will be good quality wine at the end of our journey.

Jesus is telling us that we are a vital part of God's creation, created in love and for love. We don't exist apart from God. We're together for ever.

| PLANNING A CHURCH WEDDING | |
|---|---|
| **CHURCH** | **QUESTIONS** |
| Talk to the parish priest | Are you free to marry? |
| Sort out a date (usually six months' notice is required) | Give the priest a copy of your baptismal certificate (obtainable from the church where you were baptised) |
| Notify the registrar/civil authorities | Do a marriage preparation course |
| | Do you want to marry during Mass (nuptial Mass) or outside Mass? |
| | Choose the readings, readers and music |
| | Do you want to write your own Bidding Prayers or use standard ones? |

# The sacrament of matrimony

The ultimate expression of God's love is the celebration of human love in what we call the sacrament of matrimony. A wedding celebrates both God's love and human love. A marriage is also a legal contract. This is why a couple sign the civil register.

Wedding preparations can be a time of high stress for those involved. Occasionally, in planning for the perfect wedding celebration, God's love gets forgotten or pushed to the side in the clutter surrounding the flowers, photographs, dresses, etc. This is why what happens in the church is firmly focused on God's love for us.

> Ron is an example of true love. He gave up his work as a university lecturer to nurse his wife Maggie when she developed multiple sclerosis and needed round-the-clock care. When she died in her early fifties, Maggie could only move one hand and was totally dependent on Ron. "She's my life," he said.

However, just as there is no perfect family, so too is there no perfect marriage. The marriage ceremony is only the beginning of what will be a challenging journey of faith, not just in God, but of faith in each other. For some of us, our marriage didn't work out and we experienced the pain of divorce.

# → Married and in prison

What happens when people are learning to be together is one thing. What happens when they have to learn to live some of that relationship apart is something else.

Keeping a marriage, or any relationship, going is difficult when you are in prison. Being forced to live apart can put a strain on a couple. And it is very easy if you are in prison to become focused too much on your situation. Neither is it easy for the partner at home who has to try to maintain normal life, perhaps supporting a family on limited resources.

However, regular visits from a loved one provide opportunities to keep the relationship alive and provide hope for the future.

Some prisons will organise family days, parenting days, and provide quality time to maintain and strengthen relationships. These can also be a great source of comfort and hope for the future.

## THE CHATROOM APPROACH

**C** communication – talk, write, phone, visit.

**H** honesty – be open and truthful . Don't even lie to yourself about yourself.

**A** avoidance – don't skip the difficult questions.

**T** tenderness – be gentle with yourself and others.

Our journey is not a journey that we make alone: marriage and human relationships are at the very heart of it. A God who loves us is with us at every step of the way. This is why trying to maintain and even strengthen relationships while we are in prison is so important.

Never be afraid or ashamed to ask for help to heal a hurting relationship.

Believe and invest in the future.

# ➜ Alone in prison

We can always be confident about God's love for us no matter of how difficult our situation is. Prison can make us feel isolated. We can come through this difficult part of our journey through life by maintaining and developing relationships.

Imprisonment may be a new experience for us. But being in prison is not a new experience. Many men and women have found themselves locked up. Not all of them were innocent and not all were guilty. All have had to deal with this experience and still make sense of being connected to loved ones while we and they are feeling isolated.

## ➚ Fill the gap

The words of this former prisoner may offer some comfort. Dietrich Bonhoeffer, a German pastor and scholar, opposed the Nazis. He saw Hitler's regime as the very opposite of what Christian men and women should be searching for. Although in prison, the Nazis thought he was part of the failed plot to assassinate Adolf Hitler. He was executed in Flossenburg concentration camp on 9 April 1945.

This is what he wrote as he reflected on the experience of being forcibly apart from his loved ones.

> Nothing can fill the gap when we are away from those we love and it would be wrong to try and find anything. We must simply hold on and win through. That sounds very hard at first but at the same time it is a great consolation since leaving the gap unfilled preserves the bond between us. It is nonsense to say that God fills the gap; he does not fill it but keeps it empty, so that our communion with one another may be kept alive, even at the cost of pain.

## TILL DEATH DO US PART

Joseph Mary Plunkett married Grace Gifford on 3 May 1916 in the prison chapel in Kilmainham Gaol in Dublin. The following morning, in the stone-breakers yard in the same prison, a firing squad executed him for his part in the Easter Rising, when Irish republicans attempted to put an end to British rule in Ireland.

That part in the Rite of Marriage where the exchange of promises includes the words, "till death do us part" must have had a strange but deep meaning for them.

## TO THINK ABOUT...

In order to have a healthy family, four words need to be used: please, thank you and sorry.

## Why not try...
*Saying a Hail Mary for each member of your family.*

## TALK TO GOD

*Loving Lord, while I am away from my family, watch over, protect and bless them. Fill them with health, happiness and safety.*
*Amen.*

# What next?

## → My release

When you are released from prison, life will be difficult at first. You will have to make your way with the resources available.

We know that before we take the first steps into freedom, we have to choose to live differently. Any change will depend on the decisions we make. Fortunately, we will not make our journey into freedom alone. There will be people to help and support us.

Others will invite us to remain exactly where we are or even to take a backward step. "Try some of this." "Why don't we just…?" "I've got a great scheme for a quick earner."

We have to make difficult decisions. It may be that through *Faith Inside* we have discovered the courage and strength that our faith in God can bring. This will help us to bring about change.

When we are faced with choices – and we will be – it is going to take real character to make the right ones. But if we ask for God's help, he will walk with us.

### Your release

*What do you fear most about your release?*

*What are you most looking forward to?*

*How do you feel about asking others for help?*

*Do you believe you can make a new start?*

# → Paul's story

The story of Paul illustrates that real change can happen in our lives. He was a devout Jew and he persecuted the early Christians. He saw them as a threat to his religion.

When Paul was on his way to Damascus he was struck down and blinded by what appeared to be a bolt of lightning.

His travelling companions took him into the city where he recovered his sight. It was a Christian who nursed Paul back to health. Paul radically change his life. He too became a believer in the message of Jesus.

He became a traveller and a preacher and dedicated the remainder of his life to promoting the Good News of Jesus. When we go to Mass, we often hear extracts from some of his letters read out.

If he wanted to get somewhere he had to sail, walk or travel by cart. Only the very brave or the extremely foolhardy made the kind of journeys that Paul made. Travel for everyone was dangerous. He was shipwrecked a couple of times, arrested by the authorities for disturbing the peace, and flogged.

Paul shrugged off the danger because he had a message to deliver. His dynamic preaching led him into conflict with both the Jewish and the other religious authorities. In the end, he paid with his life for his determined preaching of the Gospel.

## ↗ It takes time

Unsurprisingly, people who met Paul at first were extremely suspicious. Was he really now a Christian? People are suspicious of change, particularly of radical change.

We can expect a certain amount of suspicion when we get out of prison. We know we have changed. Others may be a bit wary. They knew us before we changed.

We need to approach our freedom and our decision to change with patience. We need to show by our actions that we have changed. This will take time. We will have to discover how to be gentle with ourselves and with others.

Coming from prison, where the first rule is survival, learning to be gentle might be more difficult than it seems. Gentle does not mean soft! There was nothing soft about Paul. On the contrary, he was tough. We need to be capable of the same toughness that Paul demonstrated.

## → Ernest Shackleton

Someone else who displayed toughness and determination was the explorer Ernest Shackleton. In 1914, just as the First World War began, he set off with a group of companions on an expedition to the Antarctic. When, two years later, Shackleton and two of his team staggered into a whaling station on South Georgia everyone was astonished.

During those two years, nobody knew that their ship, the *Endurance,* had been crushed in the ice and the crew had taken to three small boats salvaged from the ship. They sailed to Elephant Island, a rock in the middle of the ocean.

Antarctica was a place of complete isolation with no way of communicating with the outside world. Shackleton and his party knew nothing of global events in the intervening two years: their only communication was with each other.

Shackleton and five companions then headed towards South Georgia across 800 miles of the world's most violent seas. They only reached the whaling station after they had also climbed the mountains in their path. It took four attempts before the men on Elephant Island found safety. Shackleton brought all of them home.

Paul, the disciple, and Shackleton, the explorer, displayed many of the same characteristics. That is why they are remembered as remarkable men. They remind us not of the limitations but of the possibilities.

# ➔ Believe in the Gospel

We need to believe the message of the Gospel; that God loves us in spite of what we have done. We have the potential for change, because we have received the gifts of the Holy Spirit. We know that if we stumble and fall God will welcome us back.

We need to believe that we don't make our journey alone. We have our families and our faith communities to encourage and support us.

# ➔ What now?

When the Romans crucified Jesus, his friends were faced with a question: "What now?"

When we are freed from prison we are faced with the same question: "What now?"

We are disciples, just as those who knew Jesus here on earth were disciples. Their first instinct was to hide, to keep a very low profile. When we are given our freedom our instinct may well be the same.

The disciples of Jesus hid away out of fear. They had evidence of what Roman justice looked like. They had followed Jesus on his journey from Galilee to Jerusalem. They did not want to follow him onto a cross.

> I am free. What do I do with my freedom?

Our experience in prison may well have made us wary. We may have hopes for the future but the future can suddenly look very uncertain.

Freedom from prison may mean that we are now free to achieve our potential. That can be a scary thought. How often have we said to ourselves, or perhaps told others, "When I get out of jail this time I'm going to...?" On the day we are freed, in a sense, our bluff is called.

Freedom from prison is only a beginning.

It means that we are now able to try and achieve some of our goals, to build bridges in broken relationships and to get clean and stay clean in our struggle with substance abuse. And we also have the opportunity to try and repair some of the damage our actions in the past may have caused.

> There is nobody on our back saying "You will..." Instead, the Holy Spirit is asking "Will you...?"

However much we may have disliked or even hated our time in prison, it offered a certain structure that we could rely on. It may even have offered a sense of security. Now there is a new challenge.

## ↗ Responding to the challenge

While Jesus was there, the disciples could feel a certain sense of security. They could see him; they could hear him; they could walk with him. Now, huddled together in the room where they had celebrated Passover, what we call The Last Supper, their overwhelming emotion was fear.

In prison some of us might have had the friendship and support of some of our fellow prisoners. Some of us might not. But the chaplaincy team is always there for encouragement.

We know and understand the world of prison and how it works and what its strengths and limitations are. The world that we enter on our liberation day is often hostile to those who have been in prison. It rejects. It judges. It continues to marginalise. Freedom can suddenly look threatening. Fear is real.

# → Pentecost

The event that we call Pentecost changed the disciples of Jesus. They were frozen with fear but became alive, vibrant and totally committed to the Gospel message. This transformation was dramatic: for them, literally, an earth-shaking moment. The change was beyond words.

For the disciples it was the moment that they decided to shake off fear and truly embrace freedom with all of its challenges. Their lives and the death and resurrection of Jesus suddenly made sense to them.

They understood that this was what they had been called to do when Jesus invited them to follow him at the beginning of his ministry in Galilee. They understood their own potential for bringing about transformation in the world.

## → What about us?

We can make all kinds of excuses for ourselves. We try to persuade ourselves that the call to discipleship was easier or different for those who knew Jesus. We can all say, "Well, they knew Jesus. They must have known it would be all right. They had this, or they had that..."

They certainly knew Jesus. They responded to his call to take a risk and to believe.

But this is just as true for us: we received the same Holy Spirit in the sacrament of confirmation. We are also called to take a risk and to believe.

## ↗ The challenge of discipleship

The challenge of discipleship is to practise what we preach. Anyone can quote the Bible. Few have the courage to live its message. Remarkable men and women touch something within us and show us what is possible in seemingly impossible circumstances.

When Jesus knocks on the door of my heart, I am the only one who can choose to open it. How quickly do I welcome him inside?

Our freedom is the freedom to achieve in our lives what was seemingly impossible a few days, months, or years ago. Unlike Paul or Shackleton, we probably won't embark on dangerous journeys. Our reality will probably be ordinary, fairly boring and completely predictable. Yet this is where we are called to witness to the Gospel: in our very ordinary situation.

## ↗ One Church

**Which parish will be your home?**

- Will the church be big, medium-sized or small?
- How many people will be at Sunday Mass – many, quite a lot or a few?
- How's the singing – fantastic, touching or pretty awful?
- Is the parish lively, welcoming or sleepy?

**Remember!** Some parishes will have one or two priests and deacons while others may not have either. Sometimes one priest might look after two or three parishes at the same time. The best way to find out about your nearest parish is to go to Mass one Sunday and meet some of the people. Make an appointment to say hello to the parish priest or the deacon.

If you want to find out what is happening, look at the notice board inside the church. Read the newsletter. Check out the parish website.

Nelson Mandela encourages us in these words:

> There is no easy walk to freedom anywhere, and many of us will have to walk through the valley of the shadow of death again and again before we reach the mountain top of our desires.

Someone else said:

> When you know who you are; when your mission is clear and you burn with the inner fire of unbreakable will; no cold can touch your heart; no deluge can dampen your purpose. You know that you are alive.

## TO THINK ABOUT...

Do not be afraid, for I have redeemed you;

I have called you by your name, you are mine.

Should you pass through the sea, I will be with you;

or through rivers, they will not swallow you up.

Should you walk through fire, you will not be scorched,
and the flames will not burn you.

For I am the Lord, your God, the Holy One of Israel, your
Saviour...

Because you are precious in my eyes, because you are
honoured and I love you...

Do not be afraid, for I am with you.

Isaiah 43:1-3,5

## Why not try...

*Every day, when you wake up, thank God for being alive and think
of one small act of kindness you can do for someone else.*

### TALK TO GOD

*Loving Lord, let my
heart be open to your love
so that, whatever the
future might hold,
I will be truly free.
Amen.*

13

# Our journey continues

In the course of *Faith Inside* you have looked at some of the very many stories of Jesus. You have also heard of men and women of incredible courage and of deep personal faith and commitment.

Alongside these stories there is your story, a story that is still in progress. It is a story which you know and understand only so far. How it unfolds will be largely your responsibility, with your choices and your decisions. But God is always with us.

> I am a work in progress. That is a source of comfort but it is not an excuse for sitting back and waiting for something to happen.
> I need to think ahead, have courage and take risks.

But we should not get discouraged. Throughout the Bible God has revealed himself as the God of the impossible situation. If we can truly believe this, then we are free to live our lives, dream our dreams and achieve our potential.

For all of us, faith is about much more than nodding agreement to a set of beliefs. Faith is the invitation to embark on a journey of discovery. Faith is God's gift to me, personally. Nothing and nobody can stop me saying "Thank you" and "I love you" to God.

We have been on a journey together, a journey of exploration. Regardless of what we have discovered, both the journey and the discovery process continue. For some questions in life there are no answers. Sometimes it will be necessary just to live with and love the question.

# → Mary, Jesus' mother and ours

No consideration of the Catholic faith would be complete without talking about Mary, the mother of Jesus. She doesn't appear that often in the story of Jesus, but she is present at all of the key moments.

When the artist Michelangelo tried to portray Mary in her strength and vulnerability, he showed her holding the body of Jesus. She stood at the foot of the cross, watching her innocent son suffer and die. Now, she holds him in her arms. She receives him and offers him to us.

## ↗ Mary's story

Mary is a young but decisive woman when we meet her in Luke's Gospel. Our entire salvation depended on her saying "Yes" to God's invitation to be the mother of his son. God gave her no guarantees. All of the indicators were that this would be a difficult request. It was.

Mary is, in some ways, a tough woman who did not flinch from her responsibility. She was always there for her son right to the very end when all of his friends had fled. She was there at the new beginning when, filled with the Holy Spirit, the disciples threw fear aside and began spreading the good news about Jesus.

## ↗ The rosary

In an earlier chapter we looked at the rosary, one of many Catholic devotions to Mary. There are five decades (decade = ten) of the rosary – that is five times ten Hail Marys. This repetition helps us be comfortable with the words, at the same time allowing us to reflect on what are called the mysteries of the rosary, events in the stories of Jesus, Mary and the very first days of the Church.

The rosary can be prayed individually or with a community. Praying it helps us understand something of our own life of faith and how we relate, both to the Gospels and to the tradition of the Church.

If you have a rosary, pray one decade and think about a key moment in the story of Jesus.

If you don't have a rosary, pray the Hail Mary ten times.

## → Sharing faith

In every prison there is a mixture of men and women of many faiths and of none at all. Sometimes this will lead to some conflict. This is unfortunate because the very foundation of our faith is rooted in love for one another.

What does this mean in the context of our own journey of discovery?

My faith journey is unique to me. I may share the journey with others who are like-minded but ours is not the only faith journey that is taking place. Whilst loving the path which God calls us to follow, we must respect the faith of others who may not share our belief structure.

Everybody's beautiful in their own way.
Under God's heaven, the world's gonna find the way.
There is none so blind as he who will not see.
We must not close our minds: we must let our thoughts be free.
For every hour that passes by, we know the world gets a little bit older.
It's time to realize that beauty lies in the eyes of the beholder.

We only fear what we don't know. This probably means that we might need to learn at least the basics of what other people believe. Knowledge will set us free and keep us on the right path. In the course of informing ourselves, we will almost certainly discover that what we share in common as men and women of faith is much more significant than the things that divide us.

# → The call to discipleship and change

*Faith Inside* should have encouraged us on the path to discipleship and the changes we need to make if we are serious about finding God in our lives.

Making serious changes means taking risks, but God never abandons us on our journey, no matter how great our struggles.

Let's recall those words of G.K. Chesterton we read at the start of *Faith Inside*:

To love means loving the unlovable.
To forgive means pardoning the unpardonable.
Faith means believing the unbelievable.
Hope means hoping when everything seems hopeless.

Jesus is all the proof we need of God's faithful love for us.

# Some prayers

## THE SIGN OF THE CROSS

In the name of the Father and of the Son and of the Holy Spirit. Amen.

## OUR FATHER

Our Father, who art in heaven,

hallowed be thy name;

Thy kingdom come; thy will be done on earth as it is in heaven.

Give us this day our daily bread,

and forgive us our trespasses,

as we forgive those who trespass against us;

and lead us not into temptation,

but deliver us from evil. Amen.

## HAIL MARY

Hail Mary, full of grace, the Lord is with thee:

blessed art thou among women,

and blessed is the fruit of thy womb, Jesus.

Holy Mary, Mother of God,

pray for us sinners,

now and at the hour of our death. Amen.

## GLORY BE

Glory be to the Father,

and to the Son,

and to the Holy Spirit.

As it was in the beginning,

is now, and ever shall be,

world without end. Amen.

- The rosary packs the whole of the New Testament into bite-sized chunks.

- When we pray a "mystery", we say one "Our Father". Then we say the "Hail Mary" ten times and the "Glory be" once.

### The Joyful Mysteries

- These tell the story of Jesus' early life.

The annunciation
The visitation
The nativity
The presentation
The finding in the temple

### The Luminous Mysteries (The Mysteries of Light)

- These tell the story of important event in Jesus' public life.

The baptism in the Jordan
The wedding at Cana
The proclamation of the kingdom
The transfiguration
The institution of the Eucharist

### The Sorrowful Mysteries

- We think about the passion and death of Jesus.

The agony in the garden
The scourging at the pillar
The crowning with thorns
The carrying of the cross
The crucifixion

### The Glorious Mysteries

- We think about events after Jesus rose from the dead on Easter Sunday.

The resurrection
The ascension
The descent of the Holy Spirit
The assumption
The coronation of Our Lady as queen of heaven

Part of Jesus' own prayer on the cross (from Psalm 22)

My God, my God, why have you forsaken me?

You are far from my plea and the cry of my distress.

O my God, I call by day and you give no reply;

I call by night and I find no peace...

I am a worm and no man,

scorned by men, despised by the people.

All who see me deride me.

They curl their lips, they toss their heads.

"He trusted in the Lord, let him save him;

let him release him if this is his friend."...

Do not leave me alone in my distress;

Come close, there is none else to help...

O Lord, do not leave me alone.

My strength, make haste to help me!

Rescue my soul from the sword...

## THE APOSTLES' CREED

I believe in God, the Father almighty,
Creator of heaven and earth,
and in Jesus Christ, his only Son, our Lord,
who was conceived by the Holy Spirit,
born of the Virgin Mary,
suffered under Pontius Pilate,
was crucified, died and was buried;
he descended into hell;
on the third day he rose again from the dead;
he ascended into heaven,
and is seated at the right hand of God
the Father almighty;
from there he will come to judge the living and the dead.

I believe in the Holy Spirit,
the holy catholic Church,
the communion of saints,
the forgiveness of sins,
the resurrection of the body,
and life everlasting.
Amen.

## HAIL, HOLY QUEEN

Hail, holy Queen, Mother of mercy, hail, our life, our sweetness and our hope. To thee do we cry, poor banished children of Eve: to thee do we send up our sighs, mourning and weeping in this vale of tears. Turn then, most gracious Advocate, thine eyes of mercy toward us, and after this our exile, show unto us the blessed fruit of thy womb, Jesus, O merciful, O loving, O sweet Virgin Mary! Amen.

## MORNING OFFERING

Jesus, my Lord and my God, I offer my day to you. May everything that I say, think and do be an act of love for you. Teach me to see you in everybody I meet. Amen.

## NIGHT PRAYER

Jesus, my Lord and my God, I give you my day as it comes to an end. Take the good and the bad into your hands. Forgive me for any sins that I have committed. Tomorrow, help me to love you a little bit more than I have loved you today.

Tonight, watch over, bless and protect me, my family, friends and everybody I love. Amen.

## ACT OF CONTRITION

O my God, I am very sorry that, through my own fault, I have offended you, who are so good. With your help, I promise to try not to sin again. Amen.

Our Father, I pray for all the families who have a member of their family in prison, that you can give them strength to get through the hard times. Let us, their loved ones, know that God forgives everyone who is willing to repent. Amen!

H. R.

Prayer for Mum, who was always "there" for other people. Miss you, Mum.

Garry

Is it always a Christian's role to suffer? If it is, I pray that we can eventually find the light of Jesus, who led the way. Suffering is just a prelude to enlightenment.

Steve

Lord, heavenly Father, we pray for those who are not as fortunate as we are. We pray for those in war-torn countries who are in a helpless situation and also we pray for peace.

We also pray for animals, which also have a special place on earth, that they are free of suffering.

I pray also for family and friends, that we find peace and eternal life. Amen.

David

Lord God, heavenly Father, I come to you now, with my arms outstretched, reaching out to you, humbly asking you to forgive all the sins I have committed, the offence I have committed and the pain I have caused.

Into your arms, I run, my Lord.

Thank you so much for everything you have done for us all.

Until I can gaze upon your loving face and see all your wonders, can you please watch over, guide and protect my son/daughter/children. Comfort them and the families of all in prison.

Help me to live a life that reflects your love and power.

Thank you, heavenly Father. To you be glory, honour and praise, forever and ever. Amen.

Paul

Lord God, heavenly Father, I crawl on my knees through the depths of despair that I have put myself into.

I have sinned and am imprisoned. I am away from my family.

I humbly ask for your help and forgiveness.

Please watch over, guide and protect my family. Let my children feel the warmth and comfort of your immense love.

O my Lord, my God, my Father, thank you for everything you have done for me. I am truly thankful. To you be glory, honour and praise, for ever and ever. Amen.

Paul

## LOST AND FOUND

*Kevin has discovered God's overwhelming forgiveness while serving his prison sentence. He is the Prodigal Son who was lost and whom God, Kevin's loving Father, found and welcomed home. Although still in prison, God has heard his prayer and a new day has dawned…*

Trapped by the chains of my past
and stuck in my ways,
back and forth like a football
in this football game of life.
Never scoring,
myself abhorring
the chances that I've had.
People that I've seen;
places that I've been;
children who've been born,
but through my weakness, their lives I've torn.
Shattering their dreams
before my very eyes, I've seen
myself go from a loving father
to nothing short of a big time-waster.
Squandering gifts,
God's loving hand I so dismissed.
It is only now, now!
When I am at my wits' end, do I ask for his help
on bended knees, send a prayer for forgiveness,
sorrow in my heart.
"Take these chains from me, Lord.
I need a brand new start."
Tears running down my face,
kneeling on the ground,
I hear a voice within my mind.
"My son, who was lost,
but now I have found…"

# How can I answer some difficult questions that people ask?

As a Catholic you will sometimes get asked hard questions about your faith. When this happens, it can be difficult to know how to explain what you believe and what the Church teaches. Here are answers to some of the most common questions people ask. Remember these are all very big issues, and scholars have written many books about each one of them. What we have written here is just a guide to help you. Remember also that people of different faiths should learn always to respect each other, especially in a place like a prison.

## Has the Bible been changed?

The Bible was written over thousands of years and by different people in different circumstances. It's not a single book written by one person. The Bible is the revelation of God's truth in a process.

The Old Testament was originally written in Hebrew and the New Testament in Greek. To make the Bible available to people in different languages, the Church has used biblical experts. Translating the Bible into many languages means that people all over the world can read it. For Christians, God's full revelation is in the person of Jesus Christ, and not in a written text.

## Why does the Catholic Church teach things which are not found in the Bible?

The Church produced the Bible, not the other way around. The first Christians learned about Jesus through the preaching of the apostles. They didn't have copies of the New Testament. It was only later that what Jesus said was written down, under the inspiration of the Holy Spirit. Eventually the four stories about him (the Gospels) and a collection of letters from St Paul and others were brought together to form what we now call the New Testament.

Some Church doctrines, such as the Eucharist and the priesthood, took time to emerge. God is not restricted to revealing the truth in the Bible. God also reveals it through the teachings of the Church enshrined in decisions made at meeting like the Second Vatican Council and by popes over the centuries.

## Q&A

# Do Catholics believe in three gods?

Catholics don't believe in three gods. They believe in one God who shows himself in three different ways. One way to understand this is to think about water. Water can be what we drink from the tap, ice, or steam. Each of these are different forms of water, $H_2O$. It's the same with the Father, the Son and the Holy Spirit. Each is a different form of one God. It's so important to remember that God will always remain a mystery. If we could completely understand God with our human minds, then God wouldn't be God.

In life we are surrounded by mysteries. Scientists have made many discoveries down the centuries, but when it comes to the vast solar system they know very little. So much of it remains a mystery. They realise that the more they understand about the universe, the less they know.

# How could Jesus be both a man and God?

Both the Old Testament and the New Testament point clearly to the truth that God will send his Son into the world. At the beginning of John's Gospel, we read that the Word of God took on human flesh and came to live among us on earth. God wanted to show us a concrete sign of love for us, so sent us what is most precious, his Son. In Jesus we can see this love which brings about the forgiveness of our sins. In the Gospels and in the rest of the New Testament there are many signs that Jesus is at one with his Father.

There is a story about a giant who wanted to make friends with the ants who lived in a hill. But every time he went close to them, they ran away. The giant was saddened that they were scared of him. He realised that the only way he could make friends with them and not frighten them was to become one of them. So he became an ant. This simple story is one way to understand how God took on human form in Jesus.

# Why do Catholics worship Mary and the saints?

Catholics do not worship Mary and the saints: worship is offered only to God. Catholics venerate Mary and the saints. When you enter a Catholic church one of the things you notice are the statues. However, Catholics don't pray to statues of the Virgin Mary and holy men and women. The statues are simply reminders of God, just as you have photos in your cell to remind you of your family or friends. For many Catholics, the rosary is a very special way to pray, asking for the prayers of Mary and thinking about events in the life of Jesus and Mary.

# Why does the Catholic Church believe it has the fullness of truth?

The Catholic Church doesn't believe that it is the only one that has the truth. It recognises that elements of the truth can be found in other religions. It's true that in the past the Church has often given the impression that only it contained the truth. But in the last forty years it has done much to build bridges with other Christians and people of other faiths. It has focused on what unites them all rather than what divides them. This was why St John Paul II brought together leaders of all the major world religions in Assisi.

The Catholic Church believes that everyone who believes in Jesus Christ is a Christian. However, there are differences between Catholics and other Christians. For example, Catholics believe that God has chosen to reveal himself in a special way through the Mass and the other sacraments. At these important stages in our life, God gives us a special grace.

As well as this, Catholics believe that the pope is the successor of St Peter and is guided by the Holy Spirit. God gives him the authority, in certain circumstances with the other bishops of the Church, to teach what is true when it comes to faith and morals. We call this papal infallibility. In practice, it is something that is rarely used.

It's important to understand that it is not the individual man who has been given this authority, but the office he holds.

# Why does the Catholic Church say sex outside marriage is wrong?

The Church says that sex is an important part of life. It is not against sex. Sex was created by God. The purpose of sex is for a man and a woman to express their love for each other within a marriage. And this love brings children into the world.

At the same time, the Church understands that Catholics are not perfect and not everyone manages to live up to its ideal of marriage. God loves each person, no matter how much they might fall short of what it teaches. The Church teaches that no one should be discriminated against because of their sexuality.

# What does the Church teach about abortion and euthanasia?

The Church beliefs that each life is a gift from God and that no one has the right to end it. The Church believes that from the moment of conception a unique and precious life has begun. This is why we believe that abortion is wrong.

We also believe that death should come in a natural way, and not through the deliberate act of a doctor or other person. We believe that those who are suffering should be given all the help and skill possible to alleviate this. The great mystery of suffering is part of human life.

If euthanasia is allowed, then it's not difficult to see that anyone who is seen to have little value in society, because of their age, disability, or illness, will be encouraged or even forced to end their life.

# It often sounds as if there have been scandals in the Catholic Church. Why is this?

The Catholic Church is not perfect and nor are Catholics perfect. Over its two-thousand-year history it has seen scandals, from bad popes, the Inquisition, to priests and others who have committed abuse. In any institution there will always be a small number of people who betray its ideals.

The number of priests who have been convicted of child abuse is very small when you take the total number of priests around the world. When a priest is convicted it makes the headlines because of the way such actions have damaged the victims and the betrayal of trust this involves. This is not to minimise sexual abuse in any way. The stories of abuse that have emerged in the last few years have been truly shocking.

When scandals have broken out in the Church over the centuries, there have always been saints who have called the Church and its leaders back to the true message and values of the Gospel. We can think of St Francis of Assisi, St John Bosco, or St Teresa of Calcutta. Today, Pope Francis is trying to do the same.

# Why does the Vatican have so many secrets?

The Vatican has always fascinated writers and film-makers and some like to make out that there is something sinister about it. Dan Brown's fictional book *The Da Vinci Code* sold millions of copies because of this. The subject of the Vatican always makes a good story, just like the Royal Family does.

The reality is that there is nothing particularly secretive or sinister about the Vatican. It's simply the administrative centre of the Catholic Church. Every organisation contains sensitive information that is not generally available to the public. Think of the government, a hospital or a local council.

# Doesn't the Vatican have a lot of money? Shouldn't this be given away?

Because the Vatican contains much art and many treasures, it can appear to be very wealthy. But all of this is not kept locked up. It's there for people to visit, and every year huge numbers come to see St Peter's Basilica and visit the Vatican museums to see some of the greatest art in the world.

Some people say that the Church should sell all this art and give the money to the poor. But they never mention that the Church is one of the biggest providers of health and social care in the world. It does this through running hospitals, clinics, centres for the homeless, nurseries and schools. In Africa it has been on the frontline in providing help to those affected by AIDS or malaria. And it doesn't provide these services just for Catholics. In its schools and colleges in the Middle East, for example, most of the students are Muslim.

Here in England and Wales, CAFOD raises money from Catholics for a whole range of projects for disadvantaged people around the world and to provide help when natural disasters such as earthquakes or floods strike.

# Why can't everyone receive Communion at Mass?

The answer lies in the word Amen which people say after receiving the Body of Christ. It's a Hebrew word which means "Yes, I agree". When someone receives Holy Communion they are saying "Yes I agree this is the Body of Christ." But they are saying more than just that – they are saying "Yes, I agree with what the Church teaches, and has taught across the world for two thousand years." They are saying they are trying to live the sort of life God wants them to by avoiding serious sin. You can only really agree to all of these things if you are a Catholic Christian. So other Christians are very welcome at Mass to come and pray with us, and the priest will give them a special blessing at the time of Holy Communion. There are some very special times when Holy Communion may be given to someone who isn't a Catholic, and your chaplain will know about these.

There are times when Catholics do not receive Holy Communion. This is if they know that they have sinned in a serious way, and so put a barrier between themselves and God and his Church. Someone who knows this will come to confession, to the sacrament of reconciliation, where they will know the joy of sin forgiven and they can then come back to Holy Communion. Pope Francis teaches us that Holy Communion is like a medicine to make us stronger in our faith, and it is here that we know God's greatest love for us.

# What is
# a pilgrimage?

A pilgrimage is a journey to a sacred place. Not only Catholics make pilgrimages: even people in the Stone Age travelled to places like Stonehenge, where they felt close to God as they understood him.

Catholic sacred places include Lourdes, Assisi, the Holy Land, Vailankanni, Czestochowa and Aparecida, but there are many thousands of others. A Catholic pilgrimage is a journey on which God and the pilgrim walk side by side.

People go on pilgrimage for many different reasons. Perhaps they are praying for a sick relative, facing a career change or an important decision. Perhaps they simply want time on their own with God.

**People on pilgrimage:**

- are on a journey to a holy place
- travel light
- have a purpose
- are ready to make big changes in life

**Your time in prison can be a personal pilgrimage:**

- You travel towards God: your destination is heaven
- You put God first: everything else falls into place when God is your goal
- You set priorities in life: what God wants is what you want
- You make changes and become a better person, with God's help

# Why does the priest wear different colours at Mass?

| COLOUR | SYMBOL OF... | CELEBRATION |
| --- | --- | --- |
| **White or gold** | light, purity, joy, innocence, glory, triumph, resurrection | Seasons of Christmas and Easter<br><br>Feasts of the Lord, but not Good Friday<br><br>Feasts of Mary, angels and saints who were not martyrs<br><br>All Saints<br>Funerals and Masses for the dead |
| **Red** | blood, fire, Holy Spirit | Passion (Palm) Sunday, Good Friday, Pentecost<br><br>Confirmation<br><br>Feasts of martyrs |
| **Green** | growth, life, hope | Time after Epiphany and Pentecost (Ordinary Time) |
| **Purple** | penance, sadness | Lent, Advent, |

# A list of some common Catholic terms

**A**

**Absolution:** Part of the sacrament of reconciliation. It is the formal declaration by the priest that our sins are forgiven.

**Abstinence:** Refraining from certain kinds of food or drink as an act of self-denial. It usually refers to not eating meat. Official days when Catholics abstain from eating meat are Ash Wednesday and Good Friday. Catholics are also encouraged to abstain from meat on all Fridays of the year.

**Advent:** The season of the Church's year leading up to Christmas. It includes the four Sundays before Christmas and is a time of preparation for the coming of Christ. Advent marks the beginning of the Church's year.

**Angel:** The word means "messenger". In the Bible they are described as carrying messages from God to human beings.

 **B**

**Blessed Sacrament:** This refers to the consecrated host, especially when it is reserved in the tabernacle.

 **C**

**Canonisation:** The official declaration by the Pope that a dead person is a saint and may be publicly venerated.

**Canon law:** The law of the Church.

**Catechism:** A written summary of Christian teaching, often in question-and-answer form.

**Consecration:** Making something sacred. It describes the moment during Mass when the bread and wine are changed into the Body and Blood of Christ.

**Contrition:** The acknowledgement of sin and saying sorry to God.

**Creed:** A summary of Christian beliefs.

**Crucifix:** A cross with the figure of the crucified Jesus upon it.

 **D**

**Devil:** The biblical name for the evil one, a creature who rebelled against God and causes evil.

 **E**

**Encyclical:** A letter from the pope to the whole Church, usually dealing with matters of faith and the Christian life.

**Epiphany:** The feast which commemorates the visit of the wise men to the infant Christ in Bethlehem. It is celebrated on 6 January.

**Eucharist:** Literally means "Thanksgiving", another name for the Mass, the principal celebration of the Catholic community.

 **F**

**Feast day:** A day of special solemnity within the Church.

**Font:** A basin or bowl in a church used for the baptismal water.

**Genuflection:** Kneeling on one knee as a sign of honour and worship to Jesus Christ and an expression of faith in his presence in the tabernacle under the form of bread.

**Good Friday:** The day on which the crucifixion of Jesus is commemorated. It is a day of special solemnity for Catholics.

**Gospel:** A word meaning "Good News". It is also used for the books of Matthew, Mark, Luke, and John in the Bible which tell of the life, death and resurrection of Jesus.

**Grace:** The gift of God's love and help which is given to us freely, without any previous efforts on our part.

**Hail Mary:** The most popular prayer Catholics address to Our Lady.

**Holy water:** Water which has been blessed by a priest. Catholics sprinkle themselves with holy water as they make the sign of the cross on entering a church as a reminder of their baptism.

**Holy Week:** The final week of Lent, leading up to Easter Sunday.

**Host:** The wafer of consecrated bread which Catholics receive at Holy Communion.

**Incarnation:** A theological term for the Son of God becoming man in Jesus Christ.

**Intercession:** The prayers the saints in heaven offer to God on behalf of people on earth who request their help.

**Joseph:** The husband of Mary, venerated as a saint. His feast is celebrated on 19 March.

**Last Judgement:** The judgement of every person by Jesus Christ at the end of time.

**Last Supper:** The supper Jesus had with his disciples on the night before he died, during which he instituted the Eucharist.

**Lent:** A period of six weeks leading up to Easter when Catholics usually choose some form of self-denial.

**Lord's Prayer:** The prayer Jesus taught his followers to say: the "Our Father".

**Martyr:** A Christian who bears witness to the truth of the Gospel to the point of death.

**Mass:** See "Eucharist".

**Mother of God:** A title given to Mary because she is the mother of Jesus, who is both God and man.

**New Testament:** That part of the Bible which tells the Good News of Jesus Christ.

**Novena:** Nine days of prayer.

**Old Testament:** That part of the Bible written before the time of Christ.

**Our Lady:** The title Catholics most frequently use when referring to Mary, the mother of Jesus.

**P**

**Parables:** The stories Jesus told which illustrate some of his most important teachings.

**Paradise:** Another word for heaven. It literally means "God's garden".

**Passion:** The suffering and death of Jesus on the cross endured for our salvation.

**Penance:** The sacrament of penance is the sacrament in which sins are forgiven, now known as reconciliation. The word "penance" also refers to acts of self-denial. For example, fasting can be described as an act of penance.

**Pentecost:** Literally means "fifty days". It marks the day when the Holy Spirit came upon the apostles fifty days after the resurrection of Jesus.

**Petition:** Asking God for our needs in prayer.

**Pilgrimage:** A journey to a holy place, such as the Holy Land, Rome or Lourdes.

**Purgatory:** A state in which the souls of the dead are purified and perfected in love before finally becoming one with God in heaven.

 **R**

**Real Presence:** The phrase Catholics use to indicate their belief that Jesus is really present in the Eucharist under the forms of bread and wine.

**Redemption:** Being delivered from evil through the birth, life, death and resurrection of Jesus Christ.

**Resurrection of the body:** The doctrine that at the end of time the redeemed will rise, body and soul, from the dead and live with God for ever.

**Rosary:** A form of prayer using beads to reflect on the main events in the life of Jesus and Mary.

 **S**

**Saints:** Members of the Church whose holiness of life is recognised after their deaths and who are venerated by the Church.

**Sign of the cross:** A formula Catholics use to bless themselves when entering a church and at other times.

**Soul:** The spiritual element of a person's nature.

**Stations of the Cross:** A series of fourteen pictures on incidents illustrating the suffering and death of Christ and found round the walls of most Catholic churches.

 **T**

**Tabernacle:** The safe in which the consecrated hosts are kept.

**Ten Commandments:** The rules of life delivered by God to Moses on Mount Sinai. They still form the basis of morality for Christians.

 **V**

**Vatican:** The official residence of the Pope in Rome. It also refers to the central government of the Church.

**Virgin birth:** The doctrine that Mary remained a virgin both before and after the birth of Jesus, her son. Jesus was "conceived by the Holy Spirit", meaning that his origin is wholly from God; he was "born of the virgin Mary", meaning that he is fully human.